Common Sense

Lynd Forguson

R

Routledge

London and New York

This book is dedicated to the memory of
Peter Sylvester
Teacher and Friend

And to the memory of my father
I. Lynd Forguson
Teacher and Friend

First published in 1989 by Routledge
11 New Fetter Lane, London EC4P 4EE
29 West 35th Street, New York, NY 10001

Printed in Great Britain by
Richard Clay Ltd,
Bungay, Suffolk
Typeset in Times New Roman
by Mike Kelly Photosetting

British Library Cataloguing in Publication Data
Forguson, Lynd
  The book of common sense.
  1. Epistemology
  I. Title
  121

Library of Congress Cataloging in Publication Data
Forguson, Lynd
  Common sense/by Lynd Forguson.
  p. cm.
  Bibliography: p.
  Includes index.
  1. Common sense. I. Title
  B105.C457F67 1989
  149—dc20 89-6148

ISBN 0–415–02302—5

Contents

iii

Preface

The guiding idea behind this book of common sense is the conviction that the individual members of our species would not get along as successfully as they do on this earth if their common-sense beliefs about the world, and about why people act as they do, were not for the most part true. In Part One, I outline the anatomy of common sense. That is, I attempt to specify and to categorize the beliefs that form the backbone of the common-sense view of the world. In Part Two, I trace the ontogeny of common sense, showing the development in the young child of the components of common sense outlined in Part One. Here I rely very heavily on recent work in developmental psychology. In Part Three, I critically examine the two most famous attempts, on the part of the eighteenth-century philosopher-psychologist Thomas Reid and the early twentieth-century philosopher G.E. Moore, to defend the common-sense view of the world against sceptical criticism. Part Four concludes the book with my own defence of common sense, based largely on the empirical data surveyed in Part Two.

This book straddles philosophy and psychology. Its topic might have been comfortably tackled by someone calling himself a philosopher in 1889, at a time when the professional boundaries between the provinces of philosophy and psychology had not yet been drawn; but by 1989 there has been so much specialization that the scope of this work will probably upset everyone. I am not a professional experimental psychologist, and although I am a card-carrying member of more than one professional philosophical association, I do not deal herein with some of the hot topics of current philosophy of mind in the high-tech way they are currently discussed. Cognitive science is a term that might do, except that it has become associated with a particular theory of the nature of the mind: the computational model.

In particular, I do not enter into the current debates about whether 'folk psychology' will have a place in 'a mature scientific psychology', or the debates over 'narrow vs. broad' psychology, or other problems of assigning specific content to mental states. I realized early on that these would need very detailed and extensive treatment, which would be out of place in this work as I conceived it. I hope to contribute to those debates in a subsequent work.

Although I deal with topics of specialized interest to both philosophers and psychologists, I have written with the educated general reader in mind. I have tried to minimize the use of technical terminology, and when I have resorted to it, I have attempted to introduce it explicitly and clearly.

The book has its origin in discussions in which I took part, in the autumn of 1985, with three developmental cognitive psychologists, Janet Astington, Alison Gopnik, and David Olson, concerning recent work on the development of certain metacognitive abilities in young children of about 4 years of age. 'Metacognition' is a psychologists' term of art for thinking about thinking. The idea under discussion was that several of the cognitive abilities that had been studied independently by several researchers were in fact interrelated. I was intrigued by these discussions, because I had long been interested in the philosophical debate over the truth of our common-sense beliefs, and it occurred to me that the cognitive abilities we were discussing are bound up with the common-sense view of the world. It was Alison, I believe, who suggested that we test the hypothesis that these abilities, together with another that had not been studied experimentally, are significantly age-correlated, and amount to a kind of cognitive breakthrough on the part of 4-year-olds.

The pilot data, gathered and analysed by Janet and Alison, were very encouraging. It was decided to go ahead with a full-scale study, and also to organize an international conference at the University of Toronto the following spring so that researchers in this general area could get together and discuss their results and their ongoing research. The conference was a great success, and its proceedings, together with the proceedings of a similar conference held at about the same time at Oxford University, were published under the title *Developing Theories of Mind* (Astington, Harris, and Olson 1988). Our research project, as well as the conference, were made possible by a grant from the University of Toronto, through the Connaught Foundation, to the McLuhan Centre for Culture and Technology, with which the four of us were associated. Although it was not presented at the conference, Alison and I jointly wrote a paper, 'The Ontogeny of Common Sense' (Forguson and Gopnik 1988), for that book. The first four chapters of the present work are based on ideas presented in Forguson and Gopnik 1988, and follow the organizational architecture of that paper, though I have considerably reworked and rethought the views presented there, and the present chapters contain a great deal that is new. Nevertheless, I am deeply indebted to Alison's developmental and philosophical insights, which permeate the early chapters, and in that sense I cannot claim to be the 'onlie begetter' of this work.

Chapter 7 grows out of a paper (Forguson 1987) that I wrote for another book on common sense (van Holtoon and Olson 1987). I am grateful to the editors and publisher for permission to recycle some of the arguments and analysis from that paper, though the use to which they are put in Chapter 7 is quite different.

During the time I have been working on this book, I have presented various bits from it at the Canadian Psychological Association annual meeting (1986), the Canadian Philosophical Association annual meeting (1987), at Dartmouth College, York University, and the Ontario Institute for Studies in Education, as well as the Faculty of Law and the Department of Psychology of the University of Toronto. I have benefited from the discussions on those occasions.

Janet Astington, Alison Gopnik, and David Olson have been kind enough to read and comment on Chapters 3 and 4. I am grateful for their constructive criticisms, and for all I have learned from them over several years of friendly discussion and collaboration. Over the years I have learned much from philosophical discussions with my colleagues at the University of Toronto, particularly Ronald de Sousa and Jack Stevenson. I have also received encouragement, advice, and criticism from many other colleagues, friends, and students: Susan Brison, Les Greene, Robert Imlay, Bernard Katz, Ausanio Marras, Ann McKenzie, Bill Seager, Souren Teghrarian, Fred Wilson, Michael Antony, Mark Mercer, Evan Thompson, David Checkland, and the late Paul Kolers. Special thanks to Stuart Shanker, who first encouraged me to write a book on this topic.

My deepest debt of gratitude is to my wife Georgiana, whose constant encouragement and support have sustained me at a project that I would probably otherwise have abandoned.

Part one

The Anatomy of Common Sense

1

What is common sense?

Each of us has, and implicitly presupposes that everyone with whom we interact also shares, a network of interconnected beliefs about the world and our own relation to it, beliefs which guide and are expressed in our behaviour, and which we appeal to in justifying our ordinary factual claims and in explaining our own and others' actions. This shared background of beliefs, which informs our own behaviour and which we implicitly presuppose whenever we interpret others as rational beings inhabiting a common world with ourselves, is the common-sense view of the world. It is the aim of this book to describe the fundamental features of the common-sense view, to explore its development in the human individual, and ultimately to argue that our ability to make our way more or less successfully through our everyday lives depends on the common-sense view being true in its most fundamental features.

The first task is to say in more detail just what the common-sense view is. My procedure will be very straightforward. I shall not attempt to deduce the features of the common-sense view *a priori*, nor shall I attempt to provide systematic empirical evidence that this or that proposition is a component of common sense. I shall simply present, in this chapter, what I take the central ingredients of the common-sense view to be, and I shall back up my claims with examples and informal argumentation. Since the common-sense view of the world is *our* view, yours and mine, as ordinary, adult, socialized human beings, it should not be too difficult to secure general agreement about whether this or that is one of its features. It is, after all, or should be, merely a matter of articulating a series of platitudes. But it would not be very helpful merely to produce a long list of 'common-sense propositions'. It will, I think, be much more illuminating to attempt to enunciate the most fundamental, ground-floor, components of common sense: those to which we are so deeply and fundamentally committed that an elucidation of them throws an explanatory light on the most intimate and pervasive features of our everyday thought and action. After all, if we are, usually, the rational beings we think we are, then the way we behave in our everyday lives will reflect our most deeply ingrained beliefs. We behave as we do because we believe what we do. But in saying this, I have already launched my account of the ingredients of common sense, so I must begin again more explicitly.

As I see it, there are two fundamental components of the common-sense view of the world. One component has as its domain what philosophers would call the ontological and epistemological relations between oneself and everything else (including the differentiations one makes between oneself and what is not oneself). The other has as its focus the explanation of behaviour. Central to both components, and linking them to one another, is a concept of mind: the concept of a unitary, integrated 'control centre' which receives, evaluates, intelligently manipulates, and stores information from the environment, sets goals in the light of the information, designs means for achieving them, and directs the bodily actions by which these means are executed. Our minds, we believe, perform these many different functions, encompassing many different volitional, affective, and cognitive states and processes. An ingredient of this concept is a distinction between an inner, subjective realm of sensations, emotions, desires, intentions, plans, beliefs, fantasies, dreams, hypotheses, and other mental states, processes, and events on the one hand, and outer, objective, merely physical existence on the other. In what follows, I shall not discuss the common sense concept of mind as a separate component of common sense, but only as it figures in the two other components. The two components are intimately related, of course, in all sorts of other ways. Later some of these interrelationships will be discussed. But it will simplify matters considerably to introduce them separately.

Rational psychology

We describe and account for our own and others' actions by reference to a framework of explanation and a set of concepts that we do not use in connection with the behaviour of inanimate things and primitive organisms, such as insects and molluscs. When we attempt to account for some change or movement on the part of an inanimate thing, we are content to remain within the framework of physical causality. We advert to the publicly observable physical properties of the object and the physical forces acting upon it in its environment. In the case of sentient organisms, our explanations of their behaviour make use of a notion of psychological causality: their behaviour, we think, is in part a function of their perceptual input, the way the current state of the environment registers on the individual organism; and it is also in part a function of the biological needs of the organism as a member of a certain species, and the extent to which the current environment in which the organism is situated registers on the organism as potentially fulfilling its needs. It is not sufficient, therefore, to refer to the actual state of the environment in explaining and predicting its behaviour. It is also necessary to make reference to internal states of the organism, which might as well be called psychological or mental states, as mediating factors.

When we turn to the behaviour of ourselves and other people, however, we attempt to explain it and to anticipate it by placing it within a framework of rational causality, which is a particular kind of psychological causality: we believe we act as we do because the reasons for so acting are, by our own lights, better than the reasons in favour of acting in any other ways that are, by our lights, available to us in that situation. Typically, in explaining the behaviour of ourselves and other people, we advert to the deliberation, the consideration of alternatives, the weighing of pros and cons, the consideration of policies and normative principles, the decision or choice to act in this particular way, as elements in the reasoning involved in the determination of the actions we perform.

There are two broad categories of mental states which constitute the reasons, the rational causal elements, we appeal to in our explanations of human behaviour. On the one hand are what I shall call *desiderative* states: states of wanting, desiring, craving, wishing for, hankering after, preferring, or having some other strong, moderate, or weak, long- or short-term 'pro-attitude' towards some actual or possible state of affairs. At any given time, we have all sorts of desires, wants, hankerings, preferences, inclinations, and impulses, the objectives of which can be identified by characterizing those states of affairs which would satisfy the desire, hankering, and so on, if the states of affairs were to exist. Some desiderative states are more or less long-term features of one's psychological make-up, such as the desire to become Prime Minister; others are momentary, or of relatively short duration, such as the urge to buy the pair of shoes one has just seen in the shop window. Some of these we avow to others; some of them we try to keep to ourselves. Some of them could be simultaneously satisfied; some of them are mutually incompatible. We also have various fears, aversions, loathings, and other

5

negative desiderative states. These may be identified by characterizing the states of affairs which would satisfy the fear, aversion, and so on, if the states of affairs were to cease to exist, or not come to pass.

People's desiderative states are affected by their biological needs as individuals and as members of the species *homo sapiens sapiens*, by their perception of certain states of their current environment as being relevant to the satisfaction of their biological needs, and of course they are very much affected by their individual histories: what they have done and suffered during the course of a lifetime.

People's *epistemic* states, on the other hand, are constituted by their beliefs (some of which might qualify as knowledge) concerning what is or was the case, and their expectations, convictions, conjectures, and hypotheses concerning what will or would or might be the case if certain things were to happen or be done. Epistemic states include not only what one expects to happen, but what one plans or intends to do, since plans and intentions to act in certain ways include an element of belief or expectation that one will act in that way if conditions so permit. Epistemic states are affected by people's perceptual and other cognitive capacities and needs, both as individuals and as members of the species *homo sapiens sapiens*, and of course by the particular history of the individual. For instance, our epistemic states will be affected by the fact that we have non-compound eyes, that our capacity for hearing is limited to sounds falling within the range of approximately 20–20,000 hz, and so on. And if I, a lifelong resident in the temperate regions of North America, should go polar-bear hunting in January on Baffin Island with an Inuit resident, very different epistemic states are likely to result in each of us as a consequence of exposure to very similar visual stimuli, simply because the Inuit has lived a lifetime in that environment and I have not.

At any given moment, we believe, people's minds are replete with epistemic states, some of which are playing an active role in conscious life, others of which are stored away in long-term memory, but available for recall and active employment under the appropriate conditions. Right now, as I am writing, I believe (perhaps I even know) that it is the 16th of May, 1988; that I am sitting at my desk facing a computer terminal; that I resolved to myself that I would work for four hours this morning; that I have already been at it for more than one hour; that there is lukewarm tea in the pot in the next room; that if I should press the key marked 'F7' the following message would appear on the screen:

'SAVE DOCUMENT? (Y/N) Y'; that if I should press the key marked 'N' everything I have written this morning would be erased; that Victoria is the capital of British Columbia; that the sun is shining; that 'potable' means (in the language I speak) 'a liquid suitable for drinking'; that the water in my well is potable; that the antifreeze in my car's radiator is not potable.

Similarly, my mind is replete with desiderative states, only some of which will at any moment be playing an active role in my conscious life. For example, right now I would rather be working in my garden than toiling at my word processor; I would love to have a hot cup of tea (milk, no sugar). It is also true of me that I want to spend the Autumn of 1989 in China, and that I loathe the taste of Brussels sprouts. But neither of these was present to my consciousness until I set myself the task of giving examples of desiderative states of mine of which I am not at present conscious.

Given the fact that I loathe the taste of Brussels sprouts, I have a reason to decline the stuff being offered to me on that serving dish if I believe that it is Brussels sprouts. Similarly, given the fact that I believe that this stuff being offered to me is Brussels sprouts, I have a reason to decline it if I loathe Brussels sprouts. According to our common-sense pattern of explanation, these reasons will be decisive, that is, I will decline the proffered food, unless I have stronger reasons to accept a portion, such as the desire not to insult my hostess, who I believe has made a special attempt to prepare delicacies for me. But of course, if I also believe that I am fatally allergic to Brussels sprouts, I have a reason, probably a decisive one, to decline the dish anyway. Whatever I finally do, however, I will explain (if asked) by reference to relevant epistemic and desiderative states. Similarly, anyone else who attempts to account for my behaviour at the dinner table will do likewise. Though they may well posit different epistemic and desiderative states as rational causes than those I mention in my own explanation, the general framework of explanation will be the same.

When we attempt to explain someone's observed behaviour, then, we do so by attributing what I have called epistemic and desiderative states to her and interpreting her behaviour as an action performed because she was in these states.[1] We are also often prepared to predict what a person will do should she have certain desires and beliefs, and we frequently speculate about what someone would have done had she had certain beliefs or desires that we think she did not in fact have. Similarly, my rejection of an explanation someone offers of my own behaviour will typically take the form of an explicit denial that I had the belief, or the desire, that was attributed to me, or that was implied in the explanation.

Rational psychology is the label I shall use for the view that people's actions are to be explained by reference to a desiderative state, which they believed they could satisfy by acting in that way, and which together constituted their reason for acting in the way they acted. More precisely, it is the view that actions are a function of relevant epistemic states and the net desiderative state. By a person's net desiderative state at a particular time I mean the mental condition of desiring certain states of affairs to obtain, on balance, taking into account the relative strengths of all the person's various desiderative states at that time. For example, I have had a hankering ever since breakfast to go outside and work in my garden, since it is a clear, sunny day and the spring bulbs are in full bloom. But I know that I resolved to myself over a month ago that I would write for four hours every morning, and I want very much to be firm in honouring that particular resolution. So that is why I am still sitting here, clicking away at the keys. All things considered, I want to keep on writing more than I want to work in the garden right now. I explain this morning's behaviour by referring to the relative ranking of these two desires in my net desiderative state. It is also likely to be the way someone else who is privy to my authorial resolution, and who knows how much I like working in the spring garden, would tend to explain my behaviour. Similarly, in the example above, if I decline the proffered loathsome Brussels sprouts, believing them to be Brussels sprouts, believing them to be offered to me by my hostess as a special treat, and believing myself to be fatally allergic to this vegetable, I do so because on balance I want to avoid ingesting a fatally poisonous substance more than I want to avoid insulting my hostess.

It is difficult to overestimate the extent to which our commitment to rational psychology is implicated in our everyday lives. Our ability to make co-operative plans with others involves our being able to attribute shared goals to one another, and on our ability to settle on shared beliefs concerning the course of action that is likely to lead to the attainment of these goals. Strategic thinking, whether in the military sphere, in the world of business, or in the playing of competitive games, involves simulating others' reasoning as an ingredient in one's own reasoning; and this in turn involves attributing various (absolute or conditional) epistemic and desiderative states to them, and reflecting on how that attribution is likely to affect one's own beliefs and desires.

Our deeply ingrained practice (enshrined not only in moral

codes but in legal institutions) of praising, blaming, excusing, or justifying people's actions, makes sense only within the context of rational psychology. A person is responsible for his actions, we think, to the extent that those actions are expressions of what he wanted to happen and reasonably believed would or might happen by his agency. This is true also of verbal actions: the speech acts of asserting, promising, warning, and so on, which are held to express a person's communicative intentions. Our conviction that it is possible to influence others' behaviour by entreaty, flattery, bribery, or sound rational argument presupposes our being able to attribute alterable beliefs, expectations, fears, wants, and the like to them. Decision theory, neoclassical economic theory, and utilitarian ethics, and indeed the entire theoretical framework of the social sciences as they have developed during the past hundred years, are built on a foundation of common-sense rational psychology.

Our ability to make such successful use of the explanatory framework of rational psychology in making sense of other people's behaviour depends upon our being able to generalize in certain ways from our own case to that of others. We must be able, to a limited extent, to place ourselves empathetically in their situation and attribute to them many of the same epistemic and desiderative states that we think we would have in the same situation. When I see an unshaven, shabbily dressed man lying on a pavement heating vent in January covered by pieces of cardboard boxes, I have no great difficulty in sizing him up as a homeless person trying to keep warm. 'There, but for the grace of God, go I', is not an attitude of sympathy we only rarely achieve; it is the very foundation of social cognition. We recognize that despite social differences resulting from differences in cultural, geographical, economic, political, historical, and linguistic environment, and despite individual differences in perceptual acuity, cognitive ability, temperament, and life history, people are remarkably similar simply in virtue of being members of the same biological species, sharing the same planet, and in virtue of whatever other similarities in physical, cultural, and psychological environment there may be.

To the extent that two people are, and are mutually aware of the fact that they are, members of the same culture, the same generation, the same socio-economic class, speak the same language, have similar educational backgrounds, they are likely to presuppose in one another many of the same epistemic and desiderative states as a background framework that they will draw upon in attempting to anticipate or explain each other's behaviour in some particular situation. And the background framework guides and constrains our reasoning in anticipating or interpreting the other's behaviour in the particular situation. Seeing my learned colleague sitting across the aisle from me in the bus, I am not at all surprised to find him reading *The New York Review of Books*, nor am I puzzled by the fact that the battle-fatigues-and-jack-boots-clad young man sitting next to him is absorbed in *Soldier of Fortune*.

Suppose I see someone walking towards the edge of a pond in winter. There is a sign placed there in full view, which reads: 'DANGER! THIN ICE!' I am very likely to assume, among other things, that she is aware that it is winter, that she sees the sign, that she understands and reads English, that she doesn't want to fall through the ice into the freezing water; and I am therefore likely to form the expectation that she will avoid venturing out on to the ice. If she does nevertheless continue out on to the ice, then I will probably conjecture that she didn't notice the sign. If I shout a warning and she responds: 'Je ne comprends pas', I'll conclude that she doesn't read English; but if she responds: 'Why don't you just mind your own business and leave me alone?' then I'll likely conclude that she is suicidal. But the directions my reasoning about her behaviour are likely to take are in each case constrained by my conviction that she is acting according to her epistemic and desiderative states, and by my ability to imagine myself in her situation, as a means of explaining her behaviour in that situation as a case of rational action. I attribute to her specific epistemic and desiderative states which I think constitute her reasons for acting as she does.

My ability to put myself imaginatively in her place doesn't, of course, mean that I have to endorse her reasons. I may judge her relevant beliefs to be mistaken, or I might find her relevant desires wholly unsympathetic; but I do have to find her action reasonable in the light of those reasons. To use a somewhat more exotic example to illustrate the same point, if I see someone pick up a live beetle and eat it with evident gusto and delight, then pick up another and eat it, and so on, I will conclude that he is eating the beetles because he likes their taste, even though I find the prospect of eating beetles utterly repellent.

This common-sense pattern-of-action explanation is, of course, rather loose. Our predictions and anticipations of the future behaviour of others are nearly always offered with an unspoken *ceteris paribus* clause; for we recognize that there are many unexpected factors that can intervene in any situation in which actions are performed: factors that can alter, or impede, or frustrate the smooth attainment of a goal, execution of a plan, or fulfilling of an intention. We realize, for example, that intentions formed at an earlier time are subject to cancellation in the light of changed circumstances. If my telephone rings; if I want to answer it more than I want to continue working; if it is a long conversation that I am too polite to break off; then when I finally get off the telephone I may be so hungry that my desire to eat overrides my resolve to finish four hours of writing before having lunch. Alternatively, there might be a power failure, or the computer might malfunction, or the house might catch fire, or I might suddenly remember that I promised to meet a student at my office at 10 a.m., in which case I may not do what I fully intended to do, what I said to you I would do, and which you anticipated that I would do.

Even though *ceteris paribus* clauses are always in order in the explanations, predictions, etc., sanctioned by rational psychology, and even though a number of alternative and mutually exclusive explanations can with ingenuity be formulated for any given action description, the *pattern* of explanation is robust: the alternative explanations are also of the same rational psychological form. When *ceteris* is judged not to be *paribus*, for example, and a particular prediction or explanation is withdrawn or challenged, it is always because some other epistemic or desiderative state is judged to have intervened. So the question at issue when we reflect critically about our own and others' action explanations is always: which particular rational psychological account is appropriate, given our knowledge of the circumstances? In ordinary life we never doubt that some rational psychological explanation or other is the right explanation of that action in those circumstances.

It is interesting in this connection to note that Freud, having shown that the explanations people sometimes provide for their own behaviour are clearly unacceptable in the light of the available evidence, did not abandon rational psychology to search for a deeper type of psychological explanation. Instead he posited hidden, unconscious beliefs and desires, so that the overall pattern of explanation would be preserved. That is perhaps why Freudian-type explanations of otherwise puzzling behaviour are so appealing: they make the puzzling behaviour intelligible as a kind of rational behaviour after all. The beliefs may be preposterous, and the desires may be exceedingly strange, but the behaviour is explained as being a rational consequence of those beliefs and desires.

The earliest systematic investigation of the fundamental features

11

of rational psychology was conducted by Aristotle, in the *Nicomachean Ethics.*[2] In Book III, he distinguishes between voluntary and involuntary actions. Involuntary actions are those done under compulsion or through ignorance (III.i.2). An action is done under compulsion, he says, 'when its origin is from without' the agent, as in cases in which one's body is actually moved by an outside force, such as a strong wind; or the more interesting 'mixed' cases, in which one actually chooses to do something one would not otherwise do, for example because of a threat. Here, the origin of the action is technically within the agent, since the agent has it within her power to refuse to give in to the threat, but is effectively 'from without', since the action would never have been done, or even contemplated, had there been no threat 'from without'. An action is done through ignorance when the agent is ignorant of one or more of the 'particular circumstances' of the situation: (1) the agent, (2) the act, (3) the thing (or person) that is affected by, or 'within the sphere of', the act, (4) the instrument (for example, a tool), (5) the effect, (6) the manner (for example, gently or violently). An action is voluntary when the origin of the action is within the agent, who knows the particular circumstances in which she is acting (III.i.16).

Young children and animals are capable of voluntary action, according to Aristotle, since they typically initiate their own actions, and can be cognizant of the particular circumstances. He specifically argues against the view, which he attributes to Plato, that actions caused by anger or desire are involuntary, since that would debar us from speaking of infants and animals as acting voluntarily. Infants and animals are not capable of choice, however, which Aristotle identifies as a voluntary action preceded by deliberation (III.ii.17). But choice is not to be identified with desire, passion, wish, or opinion; for we can wish for what is impossible (his example is immortality), but not choose it, and we can wish for an end, but can choose only a means we feel is within our control. Moreover, we can have an opinion about anything, but we cannot choose just anything; and opinions are either true or false, whereas choices are good or bad (III.ii.3–15).

Choice is an action preceded by deliberation; we can deliberate only about things that are in our control, and are attainable by action. Deliberation also occurs only with regard to those things where we are capable of acting but our agency does not always produce the same result. When we deliberate, we

> take a certain end for granted [i.e., as desired, as the end to be achieved], and consider how and by what means it can be

achieved. If there are several means, [we] consider which will achieve it most easily and best. If there is only one means, [we] ask how it is to be accomplished by that means, and by what means that means can itself be achieved, until [we] reach the first link in the chain of causes, which is the last in the order of discovery.

(III.iii.11)

Thus, 'as the object of choice is something within our power which after deliberation we desire, choice will be a deliberate desire of things within our power' (III.iii.19).

In Book VII, in the midst of an examination of unrestraint, Aristotle outlines the practical syllogism. The actual process of reasoning by which actions are produced Aristotle calls 'practical reasoning'. His practical syllogism, an attempt to formalize practical reasoning on the same lines as his codification of the theoretical syllogism, contains a major premiss, which is

> an opinion, while the minor premiss deals with particular things, which are the province of perception. Now when the two premisses are combined, just as in theoretic reasoning the mind is compelled to *affirm* the resulting conclusion, so in the case of practical premisses you are forced at once to *do* it. For example, given the premisses 'All sweet things ought to be tasted' and 'Yonder thing is sweet' – a particular instance of the general class –, you are bound, if able and not prevented, immediately to taste the thing.

(VII.iii.9)

Thus, the major premiss enunciates a universal desideratum ('All sweet things ought to be tasted', rather than 'I want to taste something sweet'), while a minor premiss expresses the contents of an epistemic state ('Yonder thing is sweet'), and a conclusion, which is an action (the eating of the sweet food), rather than an affirmed proposition, such as 'Let me eat this thing.' The major premiss has to be a universal proposition, rather than merely a proposition expressing a desiderative state, because for Aristotle, valid arguments must have at least one universal premiss. But in other respects, here we have a formulation of an attempt to show how action can be the rational (for Aristotle, valid deductive) outcome of desiderata and beliefs about what states of the world satisfy them.

Aristotle's outline of the springs of human action might well have been written yesterday, so little have our views, and even our terminology for expressing them, altered in the subsequent two millennia. Subsequent forays into the investigation of rational psychology have for the most part been footnotes to Aristotle, though of course many substantial contributions have been made, especially in the suburban neighbourhoods of action theory, such as decision theory and the theory of rational choice.

Not only do we apply the explanation pattern of rational psychology to ourselves and other adult human beings; we also extend it to infant humans and members of many species of animals. In the latter case, verbal attributions of beliefs and desires are sometimes metaphorical, as it also is when we occasionally attribute malevolent 'desires' to inanimate objects, such as the vacuum-sealed jars that 'don't want' to be opened. But most of us are quite happy to attribute beliefs and desires quite seriously and straightforwardly to beings whose behaviour seems continuous in quality to our own. The dog, we say, is barking up the wrong tree because it didn't see the squirrel jump to the adjacent tree. The baby, we say, turns its head away from the spoon because it doesn't like spinach, thinks the spoon has spinach on it, and thinks that the head-turning behaviour might be effective in preventing the ingestion of the disgusting contents of the spoon.

There is a long tradition of philosophical criticism of our tendency to apply rational psychology to animals and children. Even some philosophers who sanction rational psychology for adult humans reject its extension to animals and to human infants. Usually this is because they take the view that beliefs and desires are linguistic states, or at least states that one cannot be in unless one has a language.[3] But the fact remains that in ordinary life we do *in fact* extend our rational psychological explanations, predictions, and so on, to infant humans and to animals, because doing so undeniably aids us in anticipating and accounting for their behaviour. And this too, for better or for worse, is part of common-sense rational psychology, part of the common-sense view of the world, which in the present chapter it is my concern merely to outline, not defend.

Common-sense realism

The second major component of the common-sense view of the world, *common-sense realism*, is, first of all, the view that the world is one: it is my belief, and I think everyone else's too, that there is a single physical world common to myself and all other people and sentient beings who are now alive or who have ever lived. I inhabit this world, but I am not merely an inert part of it, a mere inanimate object; for I and other sentient beings perceptually experience the world and thus acquire information about its features, and I and others can and often do think about features of the world on occasions when we are not perceptually experiencing them. We remember ways the world was in the past; we expect it to be certain ways in the future; we infer that it has certain features on the basis of features that we perceive it to have; we hypothesize about ways that it might be. Our thoughts and perceptual experiences are internal states of ourselves, but we believe that there is a single world we perceive and think about that is external to those thoughts and experiences themselves.

Secondly, common-sense realism is the view that the world is made up of objects, events, and states of affairs that are independent of the thoughts and experiences I and others have of it. The features of the world I perceive are, on this view, features the world has whether I or anyone else perceives them or not. The world is also independent of my thought and experience, I believe, both in the sense that there are features of the world of which I am ignorant, and in the sense that the world is sometimes different from the way I believe it to be. By contrast, I do not believe that what I imagine or dream exists independently of my imagining it or dreaming of it.

These two characteristics of common-sense realism comprise its main metaphysical commitments. Common-sense realism deserves to be called a metaphysical view in virtue of the fact that it is an attempt to explain why our conscious experiences are as they are. It deserves to be called a version of realism in virtue of the specific type of explanation it gives: our experiences are as they are because we are related through sense perception and thought to a world which is external to and independent of the experiences we have of it.

Common-sense realism also has an epistemological aspect. It holds that people have *differential informational relationships* to the world. The fact that Toronto, Canada is south of Minneapolis, Minnesota does not mean that everyone knows it, or indeed that anyone knows it. What I know, others may not know. What others know, I may not know. There are some states of affairs in the world about which everyone is ignorant. Some people believe that the earth is regularly visited by extraterrestrial beings; others give no credence to this idea. But whether or not extraterrestrials have visited the earth is totally independent of whether anyone believes it, according to the common-sense view. In other words, different people have different amounts, and different kinds, of information about the world. And they have opinions about whether they have

15

this or that information, which opinions are in some cases right and in others wrong, depending on whether or not the world really is as they think it is.

Our differential informational relationships are, we believe, the result of many different factors. People have different perceptual and cognitive capabilities, as a consequence of congenital factors, age, disease, or accident. The amount and type of information one will have at any given time and continue to acquire will also be a function of geographical location, state of alertness, interests, temperament, and individual history, including whatever education, special training, or expertise one has acquired. Two people witnessing the same event will very likely acquire much the same information about it, but they are each also likely to acquire information from witnessing the event that the other does not. Each will notice something that the other ignores; each will size up the situation differently, make different inferences, because each of them has a different perceptual and cognitive point of view, or perspective. But despite these different informational relations, we believe that they both witnessed the same event in the world.

Our commitment to common-sense realism is deeply ingrained in all our speech and other behaviour. I am not merely claiming that our behaviour, including our speech behaviour, is consistent with our being construed as common-sense realists. Much of what we do and say would be inexplicable or absurd on the hypothesis that we hold some other view, or indeed on the hypothesis that we hold no view at all. For so much of what we do and say presupposes, as a condition of its intelligibility as rational behaviour, the view (a) that different people can, and frequently do, perceptually experience or think about the same objects, events, and situations; (b) that the same objects, etc., are perceptually experienced or thought about by the same person on different occasions; (c) that many objects in the world continue to exist when unperceived by oneself or by anyone else; (d) that one can alter conditions in the world by physical action, but not merely by thinking (for example, wishing, wanting, imagining, hoping); (e) that not everyone is aware of everything I am aware of, nor am I aware of everything they are aware of, and so on.

Furthermore, these presuppositions do not merely have empirical import; they have metaphysical import. By that I mean that one does not express the common-sense view of the world if one claims, as the phenomenalists did, that the net meaningful content of our everyday empirical claims about familiar objects, events, and situations in the world can be captured by strings of hypothetical propositions of the form that if such-and-such experiences were to be had, then other experiences would be had. For example, Berkeley claimed that statements like 'There is a tree standing in the college quadrangle when no one is perceiving it' really assert merely that if someone were to have experiences characteristic of being in the quadrangle and looking in a certain direction, then one would have experiences characteristic of seeing the tree.[4] Not only does it turn out to be impossible in principle actually to construct a finitely long hypothetical sentence which is equivalent in truth-value with the original claim about the tree in the quad,[5] but even if one could do this, the claim made by the common-sense realist is not a claim about experiences she would have under certain hypothetical conditions; it is a claim intended to be about a single, continuously existing world independent of her own or anyone else's experience. She may be wrong that any such world exists, but one misconstrues common sense horribly if one construes it merely as having empirical import, such that any sentence which could be used to express an empirically equivalent proposition would be equivalent in intended metaphysical import.[6]

To acknowledge the truth of the above, just imagine trying to make an assertion about something you ordinarily take to be a familiar part of your physical environment, while simultaneously denying, or even 'detaching' your commitment to, its continuous, mind-independent, external existence. The result will be something resembling G.E. Moore's paradox about saying 'It's raining, but I don't believe it.' For example, 'We played tennis together on her tennis court for two days in a row, but I don't mean to imply that she and I played on the same court, nor that it was literally the same court on the second day as the first.' Just as the sincere assertion 'It's raining outside now' expresses (and thereby presupposes as a condition of its intelligibility as an assertion)[7] a belief on the part of the speaker that it is raining outside at the time of utterance, the assertion that you and she played tennis together expresses (and thereby presupposes) a belief on your part that you played on literally the same court. These presuppositions are, of course, exceedingly banal; but an explicit enunciation of the ingredients of common sense ought to be banal, since they are so familiar a part of the fabric of our everyday lives as thinking, active, communicating beings.

I am also not claiming that the beliefs characteristic of common-sense realism merely form the background to things we explicitly and consciously believe, as Searle has argued (1983). On the contrary, propositions expressing central features of common-sense realism are often the focus of our conscious and explicit beliefs and of our utterances. No doubt, much that is implicated in common-sense realism is usually merely part of the background of our conscious lives. It is an implicit framework in terms of which we interpret our experience and guide our behaviour, in the sense that our behaviour expresses and conforms to propositions we never explicitly formulate to ourselves and espouse as explicit, consciously held beliefs. But the distinction between those propositions expressing one's consciously held beliefs and those expressing the background framework is both relative and labile. Since our beliefs are interconnected in myriads of ways, what is a consciously held belief relative to some background network, which makes it intelligible as a belief of a person at a particular time, may itself be part of the background for some other consciously held belief. Furthermore, anything can move from the background into the foreground under the appropriate circumstances. Usually, as I walk along floor or street or country field, I don't consciously and explicitly avow to myself that the ground under my feet will support my weight, though if I didn't believe this it is difficult to explain my ambulatory behaviour as an ingredient in rational action. But if I am approaching a 'visual cliff', a chasm covered over with what I know from previous experience to be extremely strong but transparent Plexiglass, I will most probably have to remind myself explicitly that this is a surface that will support my weight. For reasons such as this I prefer to say that any proposition, the truth of which is presupposed as a condition of the intelligibility of someone's behaviour as a rational action, expresses a belief of that person. So 'I am playing tennis' expresses someone's belief that she is playing tennis if it would be absurd for her to say, with apparent sincerity, 'I'm playing tennis, but I don't believe it', or if she were sincerely and non ironically to say, while playing tennis, 'I don't believe I'm playing tennis right now.'

I don't know how I could ever hope to prove it, but I believe that the common-sense view of the world, comprising rational psychology and common-sense realism, is universal among adult, psychologically normal members of our species, though its features are usually not explicitly espoused as beliefs, much less explicitly defended; since, apart from philosophical criticism, there is no occasion to defend a view you hold along with everyone else.[8] In fact, I would say that living one's life in a way that expresses one's tacit commitment to the common-sense view tends to be among the criteria of psychological normality adult members of our species use in assessing the behaviour (and opinions) of other adult members of our species. Even professional philosophers, who during business hours may argue against 'folk psychology' and 'naïve realism' as explanatory theories, constantly offer, during their off-duty hours, explanations of their own and others' behaviour, and of their perceptual experiences, which are intelligible only if they are interpreted as particular applications of rational psychology or common-sense realism construed as explanatory theories.

Is common sense a theory?

The last sentence claimed too much. I don't really want to claim that the common-sense view of the world is exactly a theory in any full-blooded, sophisticated, explicit sense of theory-hood as understood by philosophers of science (who tend to have such high standards of what constitutes a theory that most accounts offered by scientists as theories wouldn't pass muster), or even by scientists themselves (who tend to have more relaxed standards). The common-sense view is not explicitly formulated by its adherents, nor is it explicitly chosen in preference to explicitly recognized alternative theories that have been or might be advanced as hypotheses to cover the same range of phenomena. Most of us have not bothered to ask ourselves whether we believe this or that tenet of common sense; nor have most of us thought of circumstances we would accept as disconfirming common-sense realism or rational psychology. So the common-sense view is not a hypothesis we have entertained and adopted as a result of its confirmation in the context of controlled empirical investigation.

Yet common sense shares certain important features with undeniably *bona fide* explanatory theories, though in the case of the common-sense view, these features tend to be implicit. A theory is developed in order to explain a range of phenomena. It attempts to make coherent sense of the phenomena, to account for why the phenomena are as they are. A theory does this, first of all, by ontologically categorizing the phenomena, so that they may be described systematically. For example, distinctions may be made between entities of various types and properties (qualities, features, characteristics) of entities, between entities and the states of affairs into which they may enter, between states of affairs and events. Decisions may be made about what counts as two instances of the same class of event, or two instances of the same type of entity or state of affairs, or two instances of the same property. Some hierarchy may well be posited, in terms of which some entities (states of affairs, etc.) are considered to be elementary, or basic, or primitive, or unanalysable; whereas others are construed as compounds of or constructions out of the basic, ground-floor, elements. This ontological categorization provides the theoretical vocabulary of the theory. Typically, the theoretical vocabulary of a theory is holistic: the meanings of the terms are interrelated in such a way that it is generally not possible to understand them in isolation. To understand one theoretical term generally requires being able to 'place' it in relation to many, if not all, of the other theoretical terms. To understand the meaning of 'expected utility', for example, or of 'quark', requires understanding a great deal of decision theory and of quantum physics, respectively.

The theory then proceeds to provide explanations of the phenomena by subsuming the systematically described phenomena under high-level generalizations. The generalizations (or laws) typically lead to predictions, to the effect that under such and such circumstances, the phenomena will behave in such and such ways. It may then be possible to arrange the circumstances in that way in order to test the theory, by observing whether the predicted behaviour occurs or does not. The generalizations also support counterfactual inferences, to the effect that if such and such circumstances were to obtain (or were to have obtained), the phenomena would behave (or would have behaved) in such and such ways. The theory as a whole, then, can be seen as offering a coherent, holistic interpretation of the phenomena: it provides a means of making sense of a range of experience which (in the absence of systematic description, regimentation by generalizations, prediction, interpretation), would otherwise be chaotic or puzzling. I say that the explanation is holistic because its theoretical terms are understood in terms of one another, and in terms of the generalizations and counterfactual inferences formulated via the theoretical vocabulary. They form a fine-textured network of description and interpretation

The two components of common sense, rational psychology and common-sense realism, share precisely these features with explicit, self-consciously formulated theories. The range of phenomena to be explained are in both cases difficult, if not impossible, to characterize without making use of the theoretical vocabulary of common sense itself, for the theoretical vocabulary of common sense is just the ordinary vocabulary of the natural languages we speak. But it is possible to highlight, and illustrate, the role that the theoretical vocabulary plays. In the case of rational psychology, the range of phenomena to be explained is a range of movements. Many things will move if pushed; but some things seem to initiate their own movements. I myself am one of these self-movers, but the furniture in the room is not. The theoretical vocabulary in which the categorization of the phenomena is carried out is the vocabulary that (a) distinguishes between behaviour and other movements, (b) distinguishes between actions and other behaviour, (c) posits epistemic and desiderative mental states of believing, wanting, etc., (d) distinguishes also between agents (who have mental states and the ability to initiate actions) and other things. The generalizations are of (roughly) the form: if an agent wants x, and believes that if action A is done by the agent then x will obtain, then, *ceteris paribus*, the agent will do A. The counterfactual inferences supported by the generalizations are (roughly) of the form: the agent didn't do A in circumstances C; but had the agent wanted x, and had the agent believed that if A were done then x will obtain, then the agent would have done A; so either the agent didn't want x, or didn't believe that doing A would cause x to obtain.[9] Rational psychology thus makes sense out of the phenomena by distinguishing between agents and other things, and by adopting the theoretical position that agents act as they do because they believe what they believe and want what they want.

In the case of common-sense realism, there are recurrent elements in experience that can be exploited in advantageous ways: they can be anticipated and manipulated. What accounts for this? The theoretical vocabulary of common-sense realism posits objects, events, and more-or-less long-term states of affairs. It distinguishes between myself and other objects, and between sentient beings (of which I am one) and other objects. It distinguishes between real objects, events, and states of affairs, and those that are in various ways or in various degrees not real (for example, dreamed about, imagined, hallucinated, fictitious, etc.). It distinguishes between the way things really are and the many ways in which they appear to be, are thought to be, are desired to be, and so on. The generalizations include the following: real physical objects, events, and states of affairs can be perceived and thought about by sentient beings; unreal things can be thought about but not perceived by sentient beings; in addition to being a sentient being, I am also a physical object that I perceive and think about; physical things typically continue to exist even when not being perceived or thought about by any sentient being. The counterfactual inferences supported by the generalizations include these: that ball is a real physical thing, which has just disappeared behind the box; I can't perceive it now, but that other sentient being over there can perceive it now; and if I were over there I could perceive it now; and if I were to move in such and such a way, I would then perceive the ball (*ceteris paribus*: unless it has fallen down a hole behind the box, or I am suddenly struck blind, or ...), and it would then look such and such a way to me.

Of course, rational psychology and common-sense realism are not explicitly formulated theories. They are for the most part not even explicitly (i.e., self-consciously) believed. But as I have argued above, they are expressed in our speech and behaviour; our speech and behaviour would be unintelligible – we would be unintelligible to one another – if it could not be interpreted as the expression of a shared view. Yet our common-sense understanding of the world is not merely intuitive, in the sense of diSessa's (1985) distinction between intuitive and theoretical knowledge. In intuitive knowledge, the link between one's knowledge and the situation one has knowledge of is 'essentially at the level of recognition; little or no justification for the application to the context can be provided' (diSessa 1985: 100). But our common-sense understanding of the world can be, and is, sometimes articulated and justified; and its elements are also deductively related in a theory-like way, which is another index of theoretical as opposed to intuitive knowledge, according to diSessa. If common sense is not exactly a fully-fledged explanatory theory, then let us call it an implicitly held explanatory *theorette*, identified by the following criteria of 'implicit theorette-hood' by which it resembles its grown-up cousins:

1. One's speech embodies ontological distinctions which categorize a range of phenomena, and in terms of which categories the behaviour of the phenomena is described;

2. These distinctions play an essential role in the formulation of causal explanations of the phenomena, featuring first, law-like generalizations, and second, counterfactual inferences;

3. The explanations express a comprehensive, holistic interpretation of the phenomena.

No new arguments, no fresh examples, will be needed to establish the claim that our everyday speech satisfies these criteria; nor will any argument or examples be likely to convince anyone who remains sceptical after reading this far. But some may object that even the mildly deflationary term 'theorette' is misleading in connection with a set of beliefs, most of which are seldom if ever consciously espoused, which do not appear to have the precision and articulated structure of genuine empirical explanatory theories, which are hard to portray as the result of any sort of systematic inquiry on the part of those who are said to subscribe to them, and which in any case underdetermine the 'data' which they are collectively said to attempt to 'explain'.

The common-sense view does, of course, underdetermine the data which it aims to explain. But this is true of most, perhaps of all, explicitly developed, full-blown scientific and philosophical theories as well. At any rate, I am not here attempting to argue that the common-sense theorette is true, nor even that it is superior to any of its explicitly formulated scientific or philosophical rivals. I am simply attempting to demonstrate that it *is* our shared view of the world, and that it is in pretty much the same line of business as a *bona fide* explanatory theory.

Isn't it also misleading, at the very least, to portray as a theory, or some junior version of one, a network of beliefs, no matter how comprehensive and holistic, which is claimed to be universal among humankind, at least among those who are normally intelligent and linguistically competent? As we shall see in Chapter 3, the common-sense view develops in all young children at about the same rate, and its components appear to be developed in the same sequence in everyone. This suggests genetic programming, not theory construction. Theories also typically have competitors, whereas there are apparently no rival versions of common sense. Historically, theories are typically developed, modified, and ultimately abandoned in favour of better theories. This is scientific progress. But there is reason to think that the common-sense view has been with us, apparently unmodified, as far back as we can trace the everyday behaviour of *homo sapiens sapiens* by means of history, archaeology, physical anthropology, and other systematic ways of discovering how our ancestors viewed their world and each others' behaviour.

In characterizing the common-sense view of the world as a theorette, I have not been concerned with its ontogeny or its phylogeny, nor with its distribution. It is true that *bona fide* explanatory theories typically have rivals, typically displace earlier theories, and are in turn abandoned in favour of better theories. There is no evidence that we are genetically predisposed towards any known *bona fide* explanatory theory. But though these things are true of what we usually think of as explanatory theories, it is not what makes them explanatory theories. So these idiosyncratic features of common sense need not make us sheepish about thinking of common sense along the lines of a universally held, implicit, junior-league theory: in fact, a theorette.

It must also be acknowledged that the common-sense view is limited in its scope. Unlike philosophical and psychological theories of the mind, even those which are sympathetic to a mental ontology of beliefs, desires, and other 'attitudes', the common-sense view does not attempt to explain how beliefs and desires can have the causal powers we attribute to them.[10] But this is only to say that, though it is a mentalistic account of behaviour – one which explains behaviour by positing mental states with causal powers – it is not a theory of mind, in the sense of a theory about the detailed nature of these mental states. Moreover, common sense is silent about the detailed microstructure of the mind-independent world which it posits as being thought about and perceptually experienced by sentient beings, including us humans. Nor does common sense have much, if anything, to say about the detailed nature of the perceptual and reasoning processes by means of which we acquire our information about the world, whereas experimental psychology, and certain of the other physical and biological sciences, are specifically concerned with these matters. But to say that common sense is rather general, rather limited in scope, is not to deny that it is in the business of explanation at all. Its explanations may be more coarse-grained than those of *bona fide* theories, but they are genuine explanatory accounts.[11]

I have said that the two ingredients of common sense, rational psychology and common-sense realism, are interrelated. Central to both views is the attribution of mental states to oneself, to other human beings, and to members of certain infrahuman species. Rational psychology attributes epistemic and desiderative states to people: states which have causal powers, in that they bring about the doing of deeds by the agent who is in those states. Common-sense realism attributes mental states of perceiving: states caused by features of the world affecting our sense organs, and which typically play a cognitive role in the acquisition of beliefs about the world and in reasoning. Realism also attributes other cognitive states, such as imagining and dreaming, in which the causal antecedents of the mental state are less important than its intentional object: its actual or seeming reference to some actual or possible (for example, imagined, dreamed-about) external object, event, or state of affairs. But intentionality is also an important feature of epistemic and desiderative states. Mental states differ from other states which merely exist or not, and have various spatial and other physically specifiable relations to one another; for mental states have cognitive and desiderative relations to physical states and to one another, and therefore are not, or at least are not merely, physical states. A notion which captures the central feature linking the various types of mental

24

states featuring in the common-sense view of the world is the concept of *mental representation,* which will be introduced in the next chapter.

2

Common sense and
metarepresentation

The common-sense view of the world is sometimes represented by its philosophical critics as the view of the vulgar masses, the sort of view only a simple, naïve, unreflective person would have. In the previous chapter we have seen how unfair this characterization is. The most sophisticated philosopher is at one with her simplest neighbour when she is driving home in her car after a hard day toiling at ontology. But in fact, even the simplest person who shares with us the common-sense theorette is cognitively sophisticated; for it takes a relatively sophisticated being to be capable of developing the cognitive stance of rational psychology and of common-sense realism. There are a number of fairly advanced cognitive abilities implicated in the common-sense view, such that any individual who lacks these abilities cannot be counted as being a citizen of the Republic of Common Sense.

Mental representation

In order to characterize these cognitive abilities in a way that highlights their centrality to the requirements of common sense, it will be convenient to make use of the technical expression 'mental representation'. Talk of mental representation has been much in vogue among philosophers, psychologists, and cognitive scientists in recent years. As a result, there is a bewildering variety of technical uses of this expression in the literature. It will be important, therefore, for the reader to resist the temptation to read into my discussion a conception of mental representation that is not my own. Since I am choosing to use an expression figuring in a number of well-known debates, I am deliberately risking misunderstanding. Although I will have to skirt the edges of controversies about the 'nature' of mental representation, my own use will be as denatured as I can make it.

I have decided to use the expression 'mental representation' because I think it best captures a common feature of a range of phenomena central to both rational psychology and common-sense realism. Whenever it is possible to draw a contrast between the way the world actually is and the way it seems to someone, or the way someone thinks the world is (or might be, or could be, or will be, or might have been), there it is useful to employ the terminology of mental representation to categorize that contrast. On the one side, there is the way the world actually is; on the other, there is some way the world is represented. As examples of mental representation, I have in mind such familiar phenomena as the following.

1. The same physical objects in our environment perceptually appear differently to us from different points of view, or under different conditions of observation. As I shall express it, these objects are mentally represented differently under these different conditions. In perceptual contexts, this is just a uniform way of expressing the fact that things often look, smell, sound, taste, feel different under the sorts of differential conditions just mentioned. From the second-storey balcony, the playing surface of my tennis court looks smooth, flat, and uniformly whitish-grey; but when I am standing on it scuff marks, small bumps and depressions, and a variety of tiny weeds are annoyingly apparent. It's not that I don't believe that the blemishes are there when I view the court from such a distance. I am only too aware of them, for I know that soon I shall have to set about the court with rake, roller, and herbicide. But the visual representation of the court from the balcony, the way it looks from there, is different from my visual representation of the court from close to.

In the bright midday sunshine, the meadow is alive with colour: the white of the daisies, the yellow of the bird's foot trefoil, the various shades of green, beige, and brown of the foliage. Later the same day, in the misty drizzle, the meadow looks almost monochrome: all the colours seem muted, greyed. The claret has an exquisite, rich taste; but after a mouthful of garden salad with vinaigrette dressing, wine from the same glass tastes thin and bitter. Before I step into the hot shower, the bathroom seems pleasantly warm; when I emerge from the shower the room seems quite cool, though I am fully aware that the temperature hasn't changed. The magnolia blossoms, pleasantly fragrant when I enjoy their smell in the park, seem cloyingly, overpoweringly sweet when I am in a closed room with a newly picked bouquet of them.

2. I represent the world as containing situations that it may or may not really contain. Not only do I have beliefs about the world which may or may not be true, or have expectations that may or may not be fulfilled; I indulge in fantasies about how I will live

27

after I win the lottery; in planning my garden I first imagine it being laid out this way, and then that way, and then another way. If I have the money and the energy when the time is ripe, I might actually try to accomplish one of these plans. In these cases, as in the perceptual ones just cited, there is a clear contrast between some way the world is and different ways it is mentally represented.

3.   We have wishes, hopes, fears about the future. That is to say, we wishfully, hopefully, or fearfully represent the future as containing this, that, or the other situation. We are not, in such cases, actually believing that the future will be thus or so; we are not merely imagining a possible future state of affairs; still less are we actually perceptually aware of something in the future. Yet such cases share with perception, imagination, fantasy, and belief a mental representation of some situation.

4.   According to rational psychology, our actions are not always a function of the way the world actually is. That's why some of our actions are unsuccessful: they are based not on knowledge or true belief, but on false belief, misinformation, faulty expectation. But in all these cases, as in those in which our actions are successful, we have acted as we have because we have represented the world as we have. That is to say, our actions are always a function of the way we think the world is and the way we want it to be: our actions are a function of our mental representations of the world, not of the world as it is (unless, of course, it is as we represent it).

In the above examples, there is in each case a contrast between (a) some way the world is (some state of affairs, some feature of the world), identified without reference to any person's point of view, or any person's mental state, and (b) some way the world may or might be, identified by means of essential reference to someone's mental state of representing the world in that way. The examples fall into two broad categories that have long been of intense interest to philosophers.

In the first category are examples of sensory representation. The examples listed under paragraph 1 above are all of this type, in which some way the world *is* is contrasted with some way it *seems* or *appears* via one of the sensory modalities: i.e., the way it looks, sounds, feels, smells, tastes *from here*, or under *these* conditions. Things always look, feel, etc., some way or other, of course, since one cannot perceive any feature of the world without it affecting one's sense organs, and thereby causing some sensory experience, which experience is, under normal or appropriate conditions (both conditions in the environment and conditions in the perceiver) the perceiving of that feature of the world. Many objects in the physical environment have a standard identifying description. For example, Canadian dimes are round, though they typically look elliptical unless they are seen from a position perpendicular to the line of vision. Sheets of notepaper are rectangular, though they usually look trapezoidal to us. Granny Smith apples look uniformly green from about three feet away, though frequently they are covered with tiny yellowish spots that are only apparent at very close range. Coal is black, though it often appears silvery-blue or silvery-brown. No matter how these objects are sensorily represented, a person will typically judge them to be round, rectangular, green, or black, respectively. One discounts (usually quite unconsciously, or automatically) the features the object is sensorily represented as having under some conditions of observation, for one has learned that round coins, for example, appear (i.e., are sensorily represented as) elliptical from this point of view. However, it is possible, with some prompting and perhaps some training in how to attend to one's own experiences, to give a phenomenal (or phenomenological) description of the sensorily represented: for example, 'It looks...', It sounds as though...', etc.

Sometimes, though, one judges (i.e., comes to believe), on the basis of one's sensory representation, that the world is in some condition which does not actually obtain in the world. Unaware that I am looking at a mirror wall, I perceptually judge that the scene reflected in the mirror wall at the other end of the room is an extended portion of the room, on the basis of its looking as though there are people sitting at tables in a place in which in fact no one is sitting. One judges on the basis of the quality of the sound one is hearing that there is a guitarist playing in the room the open window of which one is walking past, whereas in fact it is a very high-fidelity recording of a guitarist.

Also, even when one does not actually arrive at incorrect judgements, it may still sensorily seem as though the world is different in some respect than one independently has reason to believe it is. For example, even to those who are fully aware of the Müller-Lyer illusion, the two equally long parallel lines visually seem (i.e., are visually represented as) unequal in length. Cases in which one judges, or tends to judge, incorrectly as to some feature of the world, on the basis of the way one sensorily represents it are called (by Ayer, 1940) qualitative perceptual illusions, because the mistake one makes (or tends to make) is in regard to some quality or feature of an actually existing, perceptually accessible object, situation, or event. There are also cases in which, usually through some malfunction in the perceiver, someone will have (or undergo) a sensory representation in the absence of any perceptually accessible object. It seemed to Macbeth that there was a dagger suspended in the air in front of his eyes, to cite perhaps the most famous example. These are called (by Ayer, 1940) existential perceptual illusions, or more familiarly, hallucinations.

Philosophers have long been fascinated by sensory representations because of the epistemological problems they seem to pose. On the very plausible empirical hypothesis that our only source of knowledge about the physical world is sensory experience, and on the traditional philosophical view that a claim to knowledge of the physical world is justified only if what causes one to believe the claim also guarantees its truth, it seems to follow that none of our beliefs about the physical world are justified, and hence do not count as knowledge, since no sensory representation guarantees the truth of a knowledge claim based on it. This is the familiar sceptical argument that Plato, Descartes, Locke, and others wrestled with. Locke, for instance, used the term 'ideas of sensation' to characterize the sensorily represented. The term of art throughout the first half of the present century was 'sense data'. I shall discuss some of these sceptical arguments in more detail in Chapters 5, 6, and 7.

The second category of mental representations is made up of those which do not have a characteristic sensory quality, even though one might offer a phenomenological description of some of them in a sensory vocabulary. One may vividly imagine a unicorn, or 'conjure up' the face of one's mother; and these experiences may be expressed as seeing 'with the mind's eye'. One may remember the specific fragrance of that particular brand of perfume; but in these cases one typically does not actually believe one is seeing, or smelling something. To visualize is not to see; but it is somewhat as if one were seeing. Otherwise the vocabulary of the phenomenological description of these representational experiences would be quite different. Nevertheless, to believe that the apple is green requires representing it as green; to pretend that the toy boat in your bathtub is the HMS Dreadnought is to represent it as such; to imagine being homeless is to represent yourself in that way; to fantasize being elected Prime Minister is to represent yourself as being elected Prime Minister; to fear going deaf requires representing yourself as becoming deaf; and so on for the many other specific ways of mentally representing features of the world.[1]

The 'ontological status' of mental representations is a hotly debated topic in contemporary philosophy of mind and among philosophically minded cognitive scientists.[2] The leading question in these debates is: what is the real nature of mental representations, such that they can play the cognitive roles attributed to them by the use of 'mental representation' terminology to characterize common sense? That is, what must mental representations really be, in order for it to be true that actions are a function of beliefs and desiderative states, and in order for it to be true that we do manage to perceive a mind-independent world, even though whenever we perceive we are always sensorily representing the world as being a way that it might not in fact be?

Some hold that mental representations are actually sentences (more accurately: sentence-tokens) in the representer's natural language. In other words, they hold that mental representation is essentially linguistic in nature. Others maintain that mental representations are what sentences mean or express: that they are propositional in nature, though not sentential. Still others hold that they are formulae in an innate 'language of thought'; and there are those who think that at least some mental representations are imagistic in nature, rather than being linguistic (or language-like, with syntactical features). All of the above theorists, however, are realists about mental representations: they are convinced that something in the mind actually plays (approximately, at least) the role that is assigned to mental representations by common sense in ordinary language. That is, realists maintain that there really are beliefs, desires, and perhaps even visual and other sorts of mental representations.

Opposed to them are theorists who argue that there are no mental representations, meaning thereby that no feature of the physical structure or functional organization of cognizing organisms really plays even approximately the role that common sense assigns to mental representations. Of these anti-realists, some are instrumentalists, who allow that we are under a practical necessity to continue employing mental-representation vocabulary in our explanations of behaviour, even though there is no theoretical support for doing so. A mature science, they think, would not contain among its fundamental terms any expressions which refer to entities or events that play the functional role mental representations allegedly play in common sense's so-called explanations. Opposed to the instrumentalists are the complete nihilists (or 'eliminativists'), who argue that a mature science of behaviour is within our grasp, and hence there is no good reason to continue countenancing the use of the vocabulary of common sense, which after all incorporates a bad theory which refers to things which don' exist.[3]

These ontological issues are not directly relevant to the task at hand, which is entirely descriptive. All participants in the philosophical debate agree that the mental-representation vocabulary captures a feature which is central to common sense: the contrast between the way the world is, and the ways that it is represented as being. They disagree over whether common sense is right in positing mental representations (or more accurately, in positing beliefs, desires, perceptual seemings, and other mental states which can be usefully categorized under the label 'mental representations'). And even among those who think it is right, there is disagreement about what mental representations must be in order for common sense to be right.

The present task, however, is simply to describe certain abilities one must have in order to subscribe, even implicitly, to the common-sense view of the world. Since both the philosophical friends and philosophical opponents of common sense agree in using the terminology of mental representations to characterize the common-sense view, what I need is a minimalist, unprovocative conception of mental representation: one which drags along with it as little controversial ontological baggage as possible.

Let it be agreed, first of all, that there are mental states and mental events. By this I mean that people sometimes are in the state (or undergo the event) which common sense tries (whether successfully or not) to capture by the mental-state vocabulary. People sometimes want things; things sometimes look certain ways to people; people sometimes think the world is a certain way. Even if it turns out that what I am calling mental states and events are actually physical states and events, and nothing more than that; even if it turns out that what I am calling mental states and events are just physical states and events under a (disguised) functional description; even if it turns out that nothing at all in a mature science plays even approximately the role that mental-state and mental-event terms allegedly play in ordinary life and ordinary language; even so, a person is in a different state when he thinks that Toronto is in Canada than when he thinks that Toronto is in the USA, or when he has never heard of Toronto and has no thoughts about Toronto at all. And a person to whom it visually seems that there is a round brown penny before him is in a different state than a person to whom it visually seems that a square white sheet of notepaper is before him. If it is agreed that these people are in different states – that the ordinary-language vocabulary of mental states picks out something or other – then I have all the agreement I want or need. If there is this much agreement, then there are mental states and events.

Accordingly, I will understand by the term 'mental representation' any mental state attributed to a subject S, (either by that subject or by another) by means of a true sentence (which I shall call a canonical mental-representation-attribution sentence), of the form 'S M's that C' (or the alternate formulation: 'It M's to S as though C'), containing a representational-mode constituent M (e.g., ' S believes that ...', 'S wants it to be the case that ...', 'S fears that ...', 'It looks to S as though ...', 'It sounds to S as though ...', etc.) and a representational-content constituent C, which differentiates one belief from another, one desire from another, its looking one way from its looking another way, and so on.

Examples of canonical mental-representation sentences concerning a subject S at a particular time might be : 'It looks to S as though there is a large bear two metres in front of him'; 'It sounds to S as though the bear is growling'; 'S *believes* that the bear is angry'; 'S *fears* that the bear will attack'; 'S *regrets* that he approached so close to the bear'; 'S *desires* that the bear will go peacefully away'. If any of these sentences were to be true of S, then S would have the mental representation attributed by the sentence.

The subject in question may be human or infrahuman, or even artefactual, so far as capturing what I mean by the expression 'mental representation' is concerned. But of course, it may be that we have good reasons for thinking that no such sentence about an infrahuman individual or an artefact is ever true, in which case we have good reason for thinking that infrahuman subjects and artefacts do not have mental representations.

The reader will please note that I have not said anything about what mental representation 'really is', other than saying that it is whatever mental state is attributed to a subject by means of a true sentence of a certain form. Nor have I said anything about what it is (in the subject's head, or in the world outside the subject's head, or both inside and outside the subject's head) that makes a canonical mental-representation-attribution sentence true. I have here no theory of mental representations to offer: neither that they are *de dicto* nor that they are *de re*, neither that they are 'narrow', nor that they are 'wide', neither that they are language-like, nor that they are image-like. Nor do I have to offer any reductive analysis of canonical mental-representation-attribution sentences. I am, though, prepared to say what mental-attribution sentences mean. For any sentence with representational-mode constituent M and representational-content constituent *C,* the sentence '*S M*'s that *C*' means that *S M*'s that *C,* or in other words, '*S M*'s that *C*' is true if and only if *S M*'s that *C*.

It should be apparent, therefore, that I am not even committed to there really being any mental representations. My use of the expression 'mental representation' is compatible with rational psychology and common-sense realism being false from one end to the other.[4] But it cannot be denied that we certainly do attribute mental representations to one another.[5] And if any such attributions are true, then there really are mental representations in exactly the sense I have specified, ontologically unexciting though that sense may be.[6]

Also, in using the vocabulary of mental representation, I do not wish to suggest that I am committed to the view that mental representations are objects of some sort in, or before, the mind: a kind of mental particular conceived along the lines of Cartesian or Lockean ideas. I intend my characterization of mental representation to be compatible with alternative analyses of the ontology of mental representation, a matter that does not directly concern me here. Suffice it to say that I intend to be as hospitable to an ontology of mental representation in which we quantify over representings, rather than representations: an ontology in which mental representations are analysed as events rather than mental particulars. In Chapters 5, 6, and 7 I shall discuss arguments for a more selective hospitality.

It might be objected that I have not shown that any canonical mental-representation sentences are meaningful, even though I have confidently attempted to set out what they mean; for I have not said anything about what the essential verbs in the representational-mode constituents refer to, or indeed whether they refer to anything. Thus, the objection might continue, I have not said anything about what the truth-conditions of these sentences are, except in a purely formal way.

There is nothing to this objection, though, apart perhaps from an expression of frustration at my lack of ontological commitment. For the fact is that we confidently judge as to the truth and falsity of mental-representation-attribution sentences many times each day; and our judgements are quite frequently confirmed by the behaviour of those subjects about whom the judgements are made. That is to say, we constantly interpret the behaviour (including the linguistic behaviour) of others by means of judgements expressed in (rather: which could be expressed in) mental-representation-attribution sentences. We interpret *S* as believing that there is a bear two metres in front of him, for example, because we can observe *S*'s behaviour, and we can see that there is a bear there, and we can see that the bear is in *S*'s visual field, *S*'s eyes are open, and so on. Perhaps he even says: 'Holy Toledo, it's a bear!' We believe that the term 'believes' refers to (is satisfied by) a mental event of believing, just as we believe that the term 'bear' refers to anything that is a bear. We can 'point to' individual bears, of course, and we cannot in the same sense 'point to' instances of beliefs; but we can 'point to' instances in which someone believes that there is a bear before him just as easily as we can 'point to' the bear that we believe he believes is before him.

'Believes', in other words, is a theoretical term. It is part of a theorette: common-sense rational psychology. The theorette is confirmed over and over in our experience, by the behaviour of those we use the theorette to explain (interpret). The theoretical terms are used in constructing the theoretical sentences. Beliefs are just those mental states that we correctly attribute to subjects in true belief-attribution sentences, if any are ever true. But the same goes for bears. Bears are those entities we talk about in true bear-describing sentences, if any are ever true: bears form the extension, if any, of the term 'bear', just as beliefs are the extension, if any, of the term 'belief'.

The only defence that can be given of the meaningfulness of mental-representation-attribution sentences is given by specifying their meaning. That is done by specifying their truth-conditions. To do that requires making use of theoretical terms which have a reference just in case the sentences in which they occur are true. So if we have reason to think that some such sentences are true, we thereby have reason to think that there are mental events of the requisite sort.

Metarepresentation

We constantly attribute mental representations to ourselves and to other adult, language-using human beings. But we also attribute them to pre-linguistic human infants and even to individuals of some infrahuman species, and for the same reason as we attribute them to other human adults: as part of our attempt to explain and anticipate their behaviour. In the case of the infants and the infrahumans, we are merely extending the scope of application of the familiar pattern of explanation that seems to work so well for ourselves and our fellow adults. This extension of the practice seems to pay off, though; for by attributing mental representations to infants and animals we are frequently quite successful in

35

anticipating, and thereby in controlling, their behaviour.

In attributing mental representations to infants and animals, we would probably not wish to claim that those to whom we attribute the representations consciously experience them, or in other words, are aware of having or undergoing them, though our use of language in these contexts is far from precise. The infant screws up her face and turns her head away at the approach of the spinach-laden spoon. We say that she recognizes that it is spinach, and that she wants to avoid eating it. And we do this knowing full well that the child is unaware that the green glob on the spoon is called 'spinach', even though we might claim that she knows very well what foods she doesn't like. Nor do we think that the infant experiences her desire as such. She is not aware of herself as wanting to avoid eating the green glob on the spoon. It is notoriously difficult to attribute specific mental states to a language-less being without begging all sorts of questions about the scope of the mental powers of that being.[7] Nevertheless, it might not be too misleading and unprincipled to say that the child is aware of (what is in fact) the approaching spoonful of spinach in a 'don't-want-to-eat-that' sort of way.

Even we language-using adults typically do not experience our own mental representations as such. We have them, or undergo them, but they are not themselves the focus of our conscious experience. The focus of our conscious experience is what is being represented, not our mental representation of it. Mental representations are typically psychologically transparent or 'diaphanous', to use an expression of G.E. Moore's (1922a). That is, we typically attend *through* them and not *to* them, though the sentences attributing them to us are referentially opaque. To be conscious of something is to mentally represent it in some way; but it is typically not also the case that we are conscious of our representation of it.

We can, however, mentally represent our own mental representations, and we frequently mentally represent others as mentally representing situations. The cognitive ability to represent one's own representations and to represent others as having mental representations is the ability to engage in second-order mental representation, or *metarepresentation*. It's not merely that it looks to me as though several people are seated at tables about ten metres in front of me, when I am unknowingly looking at the reflection in a mirror wall in the restaurant – a fact that might be apparent to others from my behaviour, but not apparent to me. But suddenly to realize that I have been staring at a mirror reflection is to shift the focus of my mental representation entirely.

I am now aware that it looks to me as though several people are seated at tables about ten metres in front of me. The representational content of the second-order representation is thus an entire first-order representation.

Just as the representational-mode component of a first-order representation can vary independently of its representational content, so in metarepresentations, the second-order representational mode does not have to be that of merely being aware of one's first-order representation. I can fear, regret, anticipate, be embarrassed about some first-order representation, whether it is one that I attribute to others or recognize as my own. To believe that whales are fish is to have a first-order representation. To imagine yourself believing that whales are fish, or be embarrassed to recognize that you used to believe that whales are fish, or to believe that someone else believes that whales are fish (for example, the author of the Book of Jonah), is to engage in second-order representation.

The cognitive ability to metarepresent is a necessary prerequisite for subscribing to the common-sense view of the world. If one cannot represent oneself and others as having beliefs and desires, one cannot explain one's own and others' behaviour as intentional actions: i.e., as expressing beliefs and desires. If one cannot represent oneself and others as merely thinking about (for example, imagining, or remembering) situations and contrast that with currently perceiving situations with one's senses, or if someone cannot represent another as perceiving a situation that he himself does not or cannot perceive, then he obviously cannot construe things and situations in the world as being independent of his own and others' thoughts and perceptual experiences. In short, in order to have a view about the relation of thought to action, or about the relation of thought to the world, one must be capable of having thoughts as the topic of one's thoughts.

In order to be said to share the common-sense view of the world, though, it is not sufficient merely to be capable of engaging in metarepresentation. One must also have the ability to make at least three distinct kinds of comparative distinctions among the variety of first-order mental representations that we recognize at the metarepresentational level.

Appearance vs. reality

The first of these metarepresentational abilities is the ability to represent a distinction between the way things really are and the way they appear. Tree-covered mountains often appear purple when viewed from a great distance. Straight sticks partially immersed in water tend to look bent. Green objects viewed through red transparent film appear to be black. Because of the Doppler effect, the perceived sound of the siren appears to change pitch as the ambulance passes by. The *trompe l'œil* painting makes a flat wall appear to be a vista of distant hills seen through a vine-laden trellis. Tall, narrow drinking glasses may appear to have more liquid in them than short, squat glasses with the same interior volume. As the examples illustrate, this is a distinction one makes among sensory phenomena; it is not the general distinction between the really existent and the non-existent (for example, the imaginary), or the not-currently existent (for example, the dreamed-of, the hoped-for, the remembered). But there is also an appearance–reality distinction we make with regard to other people's mental states, particularly their emotions. The candidate who has just suffered a humiliating landslide defeat appears on television with a big smile on her face; but the viewers are well aware that she is anything but deliriously happy. And of course we must be able to distinguish between real and apparent emotion in order to attempt to deceive others as to our own emotions by the facial expressions we simulate.

Some philosophers have dismissed the common-sense view as 'naïve realism'. But if naïve realism is the view that everything really is just as it appears to be, then common-sense realism is certainly not naïve realism. Not only do we generally not mistake the way things appear for the way they are (and vice versa), but we recognize the great variety of contrasts that can be marked by expressions such as 'appears to be...', 'really is...', in everyday life. Sometimes when we distinguish between the way things are and the way they appear, we are contrasting the way something appears to normal or standard observers, under standard or optimal conditions of observation, with the way the same thing appears when conditions are non-standard, or abnormal, or non-optimal in one way or another. And of course, something can appear x and also really be x. To a normal, non-colour-blind person in white-to-yellow light, that object would appear green; but to the same person under the same lighting conditions, who is looking at the object through red cellophane, it would appear black; while to a red–green colour-blind person in the same light, it would appear grey. But there are many other dimensions along which the appearance–reality contrast is made.

J.L. Austin (1962) explored in great detail the subtlety and variety of the appearance–reality distinctions we quite easily make. Though he was no friend of the technical vocabulary of mental representation, nor of a distinction between the way things are and the way they are mentally represented, I think that every one of the contrasts he noted can be accommodated in the vocabulary of mental representation without doing violence to the valuable distinctions he made. To do so, we need only make use of the notion that belief is a representational mode. To mentally represent x as really being F is to believe that x is F, whereas to mentally represent x as F without thereby believing that x is F is to represent x as appearing F. Of course, to represent x as F without believing x is F is not the same as representing x as F while believing x is not F. So the stick can appear bent even though one does not believe it is bent, because one knows about refraction. Similarly, the defeated candidate can appear to be happy even though one does not believe she is happy, because one knows how the stiff-upper-lip game is played.

Not only does our ability to make distinctions between appearance and reality underly much of our everyday behaviour, we mark these distinctions in our everyday speech. We could not give a verbal account of this distinction, however, if we did not recognize that for something to appear a certain way is for it to be mentally represented in that way, and if we could not reflect on our first-order sensory representations of things and somehow compare them with our memory representations of how such things have appeared under various conditions of observation. Usually, of course, such contrasts and comparisons are not undertaken consciously. We are very seldom conscious of our 'perceptual reasoning'. Our sensory systems operate without our conscious cognitive intervention. But occasionally, especially when we find ourselves in very unusual conditions of observation, we can disengage the automatic pilot and transfer to conscious control: we can reflect and compare and contrast quite consciously. Many perception experiments in experimental psychology in fact exploit this ability to reflect on what is usually a completely first-order representational enterprise.

Representational diversity

Closely related to the ability to metarepresent a distinction between appearance and reality is the ability to recognize representational diversity. There are two aspects to this cognitive ability. Not only do I recognize that other people have mental representations that I do not have; I am also able to recognize that others frequently represent the same objects, events, and situations in a way different from my own. I realize that they can see what I can't see (because of our different spatial locations); but I also realize that they see differently those things that both of us see, again because of our different positions relative to the object, or perhaps because of a difference in our perceptual equipment. For example, my realization that another is myopic brings with it a realization that she visually represents distant objects differently from the way I do. I recognize that I can see what's inside the refrigerator and my wife cannot, since I am standing in front of its open door and she is sitting in the next room. We can both see the lamp on the hall table; but she can see the pattern on its shade from where she sits, and I cannot. Navigating a strange city by car, I can read the street signs in the distance and she cannot, even with her glasses on; but she can read the map on her lap, and I cannot, unless I put my glasses on. She can frequently identify by its fragrance the brand of perfume someone is wearing, whereas to me, it either 'smells nice' or it doesn't.

If I couldn't metarepresent these sorts of representational diversity, I couldn't believe, as I do, that the same things look and smell differently to different people; I couldn't believe, as I do, that the features these things have are quite independent of my own sensory representations of them at some particular moment. Nor would I be able to explain why my wife can't tell what's printed on the street sign when I find it so clearly legible.

Perceptual diversity is not the only kind of representational diversity one must be able to recognize to be a rational psychologist or a common-sense realist. I must take cognizance of the fact that others frequently know things that I don't know (and therefore represent things that I don't represent), and also that they have knowledge that I don't have about some of the same things, events, and situations about which we both have some knowledge (and therefore they represent them differently from the way I do). What holds for knowledge holds also for belief. Not only do I recognize that people have different beliefs, I frequently judge them to have false beliefs on topics about which I think I am in the know. I can even acknowledge that some of my own beliefs are false, though of course if I had any idea which beliefs these are, I wouldn't hold them any longer. Again, I recognize from their behaviour that others have different desires from my own, and that sometimes these are in conflict with my own. Even when I have reason to believe that I share a common goal with someone else, we differ in the actions we tend to take to achieve the goal, and this leads me to attribute to them beliefs different from my own about effective or appropriate means to realize our mutual aim. I also recognize that people's emotional reactions to situations and events may be different from my own. When it was announced that Oxford University had declined to award Prime Minister Margaret Thatcher an honorary degree, Mrs Thatcher's emotional representation of the situation was no doubt different from that of the leader of the Labour Party.

To recognize representational diversity is not merely to acknowledge that others perceive and think about things differently; it is also frequently to acknowledge that their representations of the world are better, more adequate to the way the world is, than one's own, in the sense that they are more truly indicative of how things stand, and also in the sense that they are more appropriate to the way things stand (for example, in the case of our different desires). But it is also, of course, often to be convinced that one's own representation of how things stand is better, more adequate, than theirs.

The ability to recognize representational diversity clearly underlies our conviction, central to common-sense realism, that there is a single world common to all sentient beings, the features of which are independent of the representations any of them may have of it. It also underpins our ability to explain and anticipate the actions of others by attributing to them beliefs and desires that we do not share. The recognition of representational diversity is especially important in explaining those unsuccessful actions of others (and of oneself) which require us to ascribe a false belief to the other (or to one's own earlier self). Closely related to this is the type of strategic thinking required in competitive games, in which one must try to simulate someone else's likely pattern of thought in order to ensure that certain of their actions will be unsuccessful, and that one's own actions will be successful. In playing chess, for example, I must try to figure out what my opponent is trying to accomplish, so that I may take measures to frustrate her aims.

Representational change

The ability to recognize representational change is the third cognitive ability, underlying the common-sense view of the world, which requires making comparative distinctions among mental representations. One's first-order representations change all the time, of course. I used to be afraid of dogs, but now I am at ease when encountering a strange dog. I used to be able to read without spectacles, but I can no longer do so. Not only do my sensory representations change as I alter the location of my body, the orientation of my eyes and of my head, and so on; I represent things differently by acquiring new beliefs, whether these be true ones or false ones. My overall representation of the world is continually 'updated' in the light of every new belief I acquire. Not only are new beliefs added to the 'data base'; old ones are continually being deleted. The squirrel who had been living in my attic and raiding my bird feeder I had assumed was a male, whom I called Rotten Ralph. After I trapped Ralph (for enforced transportation to a distant forest) I discovered that Ralph is really a female who had recently given birth. So now I not only believe that Rotten Ralph is a female; I also believe that I have baby squirrels in my attic. My first-order desires also undergo change, both in the short term and over a longer period, often in gradual ways. Early this morning I wanted a cup of coffee. So I drank one. In fact, over the past two hours I have had three cups of coffee, and now I have no desire for any more.

In reporting examples of representational change in myself, I thereby acknowledge my recognition of representational change. But to do that I not only have to metarepresent certain of my present representations (what I now believe, want, fear); I also have to metarepresent simultaneously my earlier representations on the same 'topics', and I have to recognize that they are now different from what they were then. If I could not do this, I would be unable to recognize that I have ever changed my mind about anything.

I not only recognize representational change in myself; I also attribute it to others. People lose, and sometimes regain, their religious beliefs. My neighbour was startled for an instant yesterday when he saw (what was in fact) a portion of my garden hose in the long grass; he thought it was a snake, but quickly recognized it for what it was. Yesterday he was eager to play golf with me today; but when I talked with him this morning, the prospect had palled.

It is thus an exceedingly important, albeit an utterly banal, feature of our cognitive lives that our representations change, and that we recognize this. Most of the time, our exploitation of our understanding of representational diversity and representational change is automatic: we automatically metarepresent in accomplishing this or that behavioural task without the least amount of awareness that we are doing so. But from time to time, control must be exercised; we need to take cognizance of the situation we are in and consciously take account of first-order representations on our own part, or consciously attribute them to others. When I have mislaid something, for instance, I need to try self-consciously to remember what I was doing when I last had the thing to hand. When the bookshop telephones to say that the book

I ordered six months ago has finally arrived, I recall that I did desperately want it then, though I am irked at having agreed in advance to purchase something about which I am now utterly indifferent.

The ability to metarepresent, the ability to represent distinctions between appearance and reality, the ability to recognize representational diversity and representational change: these are all embedded at the heart of the common-sense view of the world, as I have attempted to show in detail in this chapter. What is surprising is the fact that although these abilities are probably universal among human adults of normal intelligence, they are absent in young children. Even after the stage at which linguistic development is fairly advanced, some of these metarepresentational abilities have yet to appear. Tracing the development of these abilities is the task of the next chapter.

Part two

The Ontogeny of Common Sense

3

The origins of common sense:
from birth to age four

The cognitive abilities of very young children are difficult to study. Either they have not yet begun to use language at all, or their command of it is still rudimentary in comparison to an adult, or even a 6-year-old. A sufficient condition for attributing the mastery of a certain cognitive concept to an adult, fluent language-user is the consistent, appropriate use of the word(s), phrase(s), or grammatical construction(s) associated with that concept. A person who uses the subjunctive conditional appropriately, for example, demonstrates thereby her mastery of the concept of the counterfactual. Similarly, someone who uses words such as 'thinks' or 'believes' appropriately demonstrates thereby his understanding of the concept of belief. But if the child has no vocabulary, or doesn't use the appropriate words in the appropriate way, that alone does not prove that the child lacks the concept in question.

It is, however, extremely difficult to devise non-linguistic tasks in which conditions indicative of understanding a certain cognitive concept can be systematically manipulated. Perhaps for that reason, many of the early studies of very young children were naturalistic: children were observed in naturalistic settings in which cognitive competencies of various sorts are likely to be exhibited spontaneously. Sometimes, a number of children were followed longitudinally over several months or years, and the emergence of various types of behaviour, especially speech behaviour, was noted. But the mere fact that a child uses the words, even uses them appropriately in some contexts, does not mean that she has mastered the concept, if there are other important linguistic contexts crucial to demonstration of understanding where the word (phrase, construction) has not yet been used.

Thus, it should come as no surprise to learn that there is considerable controversy among researchers in cognitive development over the question of when certain important

47

cognitive abilities make their first appearance. After children have completed their second year, it becomes progressively easier to study them by means of experimental techniques keyed to their linguistic ability, and there is accordingly less controversy about the developmental history. But widely different claims have been made in recent years about the first appearance of a concept of mind in young children from earliest infancy until the age of about 2 years. Since having a concept of mind (i.e., having the concept of oneself and others as having mental states, as perceiving and thinking various things) seems clearly to require the ability to metarepresent one's own and others' mental representations, it will be necessary to enter into this controversy somewhat, since it is the task of the present chapter to trace the origins of common sense, and that means locating the first appearance of the ability to metarepresent, and also of the ability to distinguish appearance from reality, to recognize representational diversity and representational change. The procedure will be to survey some of the signal accomplishments of the first two years or so of life, accomplishments that have been cited by some researchers as evidence for attributing metarepresentational ability. Following this survey, I shall formulate a criterion for attributing metarepresentational prowess, and then apply the criterion to the data, with the aim of identifying the earliest age (approximate to within a few months) at which it would be unreasonable to refuse to ascribe metarepresentational ability to the child.

From birth to eighteen months

According to the epistemological empiricism of John Locke (1894), the mind of the newborn infant is a *tabula rasa*, which becomes organized and structured by experiential input. The only innate mental structure, for Locke and other early modern empiricists, is a natural tendency to associate similar experiences (ideas) together, so that the child comes to build up knowledge of natural kinds, of causal regularities, and so on. At the beginning of the present century, essentially this same 'radical empiricism' was still the received view in both philosophy and the fledgling field of psychology, as evidenced by William James's famous dictum that at birth, the mind of the child is a 'blooming, buzzing confusion'. It is now known, though, that the mind of the neonate is highly organized to process incoming sensory experience in certain ways. Newborn infants can visually recognize the real shape of a rectangle at various orientations, when its retinal image is highly variable, for example. Furthermore, extremely young infants recognize human faces and their mother's voice. At the very beginning of life, the infant mentally represents aspects of its environment. But these representations are responses to input from the environment: the representational content is constrained by the perceptual input and whatever innate or recently acquired structures there are for processing perceptual input. But there is no evidence that newborn infants generate mental representations of hypothetical or counterfactual situations.

Between 9 and 12 months of age, infants begin to behave in ways that invite metarepresentational description. That is, we can observe them exhibiting behaviour that we would describe using metarepresentational vocabulary if the behaviour were exhibited by an adult; so it is tempting to interpret the infants' behaviour as expressing metarepresentational abilities. This may be over-generous, however, just as our tendency to interpret the behaviour of cats, dogs, and other familiar animals as expressing sophisticated propositional attitudes, may be an over-generous anthro-pomorphism. A more cautious strategy to apply to infants, as well as to animals, would be to attribute those intentional states which make for the most reasonable explanation of the behaviour as a case of intentional action (i.e., as intentionally guided behaviour), if we already have reason to think that the behaviour in question is an action. To adopt this strategy is to make use of what Dennett (1978, 1987) calls 'the intentional stance' in describing and explaining behaviour, as opposed to the 'physical stance', which attempts to describe and explain the infant's behaviour as the movements of a purely physical system in purely physical terms (for example, the laws of mechanics), and the 'design stance', which attempts to explain the same behaviour as the optimal execution of a programme or routine that the system is designed to execute. If the behaviour is unintelligible unless one attributes to it beliefs, desires, goals, and intentions, and is explainable and predictable if one does make these attributions, then, Dennett argues, the attributions are justified.

This strategy can also be seen as an employment of the 'principle of charity' used by Davidson's (1984) radical interpreters, who have the task of interpreting the utterances of people whose language is totally alien from their own. The principle of charity instructs the interpreter to attribute as many of the interpreter's own beliefs to the speakers as is necessary to render their speech behaviour interpretable as the meaningful utterances of rational beings. If we try to construe the infants' gestures, verbal behaviour, and other behaviour as the rational actions of members of an alien tribe, trying to communicate with us, trying to solve some of the same life problems we face (for example, getting others to assist them in achieving their goals), and attribute to them those beliefs and other mental representations which render them interpretable as fellow rational creatures (though limited in their knowledge, power, and in other respects), we may hope to find the point at which metarepresentation appears: namely, the point at which they begin to exhibit behaviour that we cannot reasonably interpret as minimally rational creatures trying to achieve their ends without attributing to them the ability to represent themselves or others as having mental representations.

At about 9 months, children begin to use a toy as a topic for social play with others (Trevarthen 1980; Trevarthen and Hubley 1979). At about the same time the infant begins to look at what its mother is looking at (Scaife and Bruner 1975). This indicates a capacity for shared attention and reference, which Bruner (1975) has proposed as a precondition for the capacity for joint action and verbal dialogue. Between 9 and 12 months, a child will follow the pointing gestures of adults; it also points to objects itself, obeys rudimentary verbal or gestural requests, and begins to make gestural requests for adults to obtain objects for it (Lempers, Flavell, and Flavell 1977; Bretherton, McNew, and Beeghly-Smith 1981).

Are these infants metarepresenters? Are they forming second-order representations of their own and others' representations? Bretherton *et al.* (1981) claim that this behaviour shows that the 9–12-month-old infant has acquired a knowledge 'of others and of oneself as a psychological agent with intentions, beliefs, emotions, and the ability to communicate'. Bretherton and Beeghly (1982) have argued that this early behaviour is evidence of intentional communication, defined by Bates *et al.* (1975) as 'a priori awareness of the effect that the message is designed to have on an addressee', and this in turn indicates that even 9-month-old infants have an implicit theory of mind. But as Perner (1988b) has pointed out, the designed effect in question can be understood as some behaviour on the part of the addressee. There is insufficient reason to attribute to the infant any awareness of, or aim to produce, an effect of believing something or of intending to perform some act (i.e., some mental state). Only if we can reasonably attribute to the 9–12-month-old infant the awareness of, and the goal of producing, the latter sort of effect in the addressee should we say that the infant is representing the addressee as having mental representations. Bretherton and Beeghly (1982) seem to concede this point, when they say: 'It is not suggested that infants can reflect on their own or others' inner states; we merely suggest that they possess a theory of mind in the same sense that a 4-year-old possesses and uses grammatical rules that she or he cannot verbalize.' This is evidently attribution of an implicit theory of mind on the same grounds that linguists such as Chomsky (1980) attribute an implicit, 'procedural' knowledge of a grammar (a theory which relates patterns of sound and meanings) to anyone whose behaviour exhibits competence in the language described (i.e., generated) by the grammar, even in the absence of any explicit, 'declarative' knowledge of the grammar.

Early communicative behaviour does, however, indicate the possession of some concept of agency: the ability of a being to initiate its own behaviour. At 4 months, infants treat animate objects merely as passive things which they attempt to control (Poulin-Dubois and Shultz 1988); but by the time they are beginning to speak, they make use of the agentive case, indicating some implicit awareness of animate beings performing their own actions (Bloom, Lightbown, and Hood 1975; Bowerman 1976; Brown 1973; and Slobin 1970).

Bretherton *et al.* (1981) report the use of words referring to the 'internal states' of self and others in infants as young as 11 months ('see' and 'look'), and of utterances about the causes and effects of the internal states of self and others by 17 months (self: 'Head-ouch-cut'; other: 'Baby hurt'). But although the conversational use of these words by very young children can be construed as having mental reference (for example, according to the Cartesian view that whereas the bodily damage is physical, the resulting pain is mental), it is more reasonable to interpret them as reporting, or attributing, an internal physical condition.

Eighteen months to three years

Much more revealing are some of the one-word speech acts of 18-month-old children. The words used by children at this stage sound like words in the adult vocabulary, but they are often used by infant speakers with special, infant meanings. Often the same 'word' will have a variety of meanings, depending on the context of utterance, these meanings reflecting the cognitive concerns of the child rather than the semantic structure of adult language, as Gopnik and Meltzoff found in their extensive study of the speech of 18-month-old children (Gopnik 1982, 1984a, 1984b, Gopnik and Meltzoff 1984, 1985a, 1985b, 1985c, 1986, 1987). Children at this age use 'adult' words to designate aspects of plans (actions performed on objects to bring about goals): their completion ('there'), failure ('no'), or repetition ('more') (Gopnik 1982).

Infants show the ability to form plans at about 12 months, but their ability to reflect on their plans, to represent them, appears only at about 18 months, as evidenced by their use of these words in this way (Gopnik 1984a). The ability to reflect on one's plans requires the ability to form 'hypothetical' representations, enabling the child to imagine possible specific events and states of affairs. These hypothetical representations can 'override' their representations of the currently perceived environment (Gopnik and Meltzoff 1985). At this stage, young children are clearly producing mental representations (psychological attitudes with representational content): they are representing situations as desired, or as planned. The use of these words to indicate success (completion) and failure also shows that these children have acquired some understanding of means–end relationships, just as their use of 'gone' at this age to encode the concept of something that exists but is not currently perceived, reflects their understanding of the concept of an object with its own continuing identity even when it is not perceived (Gopnik and Meltzoff 1985c; 1986).

During this same period, the concept of an animate agent, as opposed to an inanimate object, or perhaps of which familiar objects are animate and which inanimate, is consolidated. At 16 months, children do not react with surprise, either emotionally or by appropriate motor movements, to a chair that appears to move on its own, whereas by 24 months they do (Golinkoff and Harding 1980). Thus crucial components of common-sense psychology (the understanding of means–end relationships, and of the difference between animate agents and passive inanimate objects, central to the concept of intentional action) and of common-sense realism (the concept of an object continuing to exist unperceived) seem to be acquired at about the same time.

This plan-encoding use of these words appears to be the middle stage in a three-stage sequence in the use of these same words, all appearing at about 18 months (Gopnik and Meltzoff 1985a). In the first, social stage, 'there' is used to draw the attention of another to an object, 'no 'is used to refuse suggestions, and 'more' is used to request assistance. In the third stage, 'there' is used to indicate the location of an object, 'more' is used to indicate similarity between objects, and 'no' is used as a rudimentary propositional negation. A child will, for instance, look at a bare-headed doll and say 'No hat on'.

At 18 months, then, a child's behaviour is clearly being guided by its representation of objects and events that are not currently being perceived. But this 'insightful' behaviour requires only first-order representations. A plan, for example, is in these cases no more than a represented possible future state of affairs which the infant wants to obtain and is trying to (or has failed to) bring about. There is no suggestion that the infant represents a representational state of himself or another. There is, therefore, no compelling reason to ascribe metarepresentational prowess to children this age on the basis of many of the accomplishments studied by Gopnik and Meltzoff. On the other hand, using 'no' to comment on one's unsuccessful plans might well be thought to presuppose the metarepresentation of one's own planned outcome as unfulfilled; and using 'no' to assert that the doll does not have a hat on might well be thought to require the ability to represent a situation in which the doll has a hat on and to compare it with the situation that actually obtains.

At about the same age, between 18 months and 2 years, children begin to engage in pretence, and they recognize pretence in others (Piaget 1951). The child will pretend, for example, that a banana is a telephone, and will happily go along with her mother's game of pretending that the banana is a telephone. Slightly later, between 24 and 32 months, children begin to pretend to have feelings they don't really have (Dunn, Bretherton, and Munn 1987), and 28-month-old children who use the words 'pretend' and 'real' do so to contrast make-believe with reality, especially regarding monsters (Bretherton and Beeghly 1982). Leslie (1987, 1988) has argued that the ability to engage in and recognize pretence requires metarepresentation, for the child must represent the banana as a telephone while at the same time representing it as a banana. The child doesn't actually believe that the banana is a telephone; she doesn't confuse the two concepts of banana and telephone together. She is capable of treating it as a banana, then without hesitation move into the pretend mode, with banana held to ear, and so on, then 'exit' the pretend mode and immediately go on to peel the banana and eat it. In fact, pretence behaviour is signalled by characteristic mannerisms, including a certain intonation of voice, exaggerated gestures, and 'knowing' looks, so that others will know that one is pretending, and will know that one knows that one is (only) pretending. As Leslie (1987) puts it, to do this, the child must be able to 'decouple' the representation of the object which it knows is a banana from its usual perceptual input and behavioural output conditions and use it in this special way. If one were not able to mentally represent oneself or one's playmate as merely pretending that the banana is a telephone, then pretence behaviour, especially co-operative pretence behaviour, would be impossible. As Russell (1988) says, the child who engages in pretence implicitly recognizes a basic asymmetry between actual situations and our mental representations of them. So here we have a fairly compelling case for ascribing metarepresentational ability to young children; the child's pretence behaviour is interpretable as rational action only by attributing to her the capacity to form representations of her own and others' representations.

Between the ages of two and three, we can see several aspects of the common-sense view of the world beginning to take shape. It is not always clear, however, which of the abilities that develop during this period involve metarepresentation. At around the age of two, children begin expressing intentions linguistically, by means of words such as 'gonna' and 'hafta' (Shultz 1980). Shortly thereafter, their earliest 'why' questions show their ability to refer to their own and others' intentions, and by the time they are three (Shatz, Wellman, and Silber (1983) report – they do not cite any examples) they linguistically contrast actions actually performed by themselves and others with what was intended. During their third year children also begin to make interpretative comments on their own and others' mental states, for example in order to direct or explain behaviour; they comment on their own and someone else's expected and past experiences, and discuss how their own or another's mental state might be changed, or what caused it (Bretherton and Beeghly 1982; Dunn, Bretherton, and Munn 1987). In fact, the concept of psychological causality is much more salient for young children than that of physical causality, as measured by the frequency and appropriateness of their causal utterances during this period (Hood and Bloom 1979).

Shultz (Wells and Shultz 1980; Poulin-Dubois and Shultz 1988) has identified several rules adults use for judging the intentionality of someone else's action outcome. If one has been informed about what a person's intention was, one can use the 'matching' rule to see whether the outcome matches the known intention. But if the other person's intention is not already known, three 'objective' rules are available. The 'discounting' rule directs one to discount an 'internal' cause such as an intention whenever it is obvious that an external cause accounts for the outcome. (If you can see that I was tripped, then you will discount the possibility that I fell intentionally.) According to the 'valence' rule, an outcome which is emotionally 'positive' for the agent is held to have been intended, whereas 'negative' outcomes are unintended. The 'monitoring' rule says that if a person is obviously monitoring his own actions, then he is controlling them, and hence is acting intentionally. Three-year-old children make use of the matching rule, but if only objective rules are available to them, they tend to judge all outcomes as intentional (Shultz 1988). Children begin to make use of the discounting strategy at age 4 (Wells and Shultz 1980), and of the valence and monitoring strategies at 5 (Smith 1978); but the matching rule always overrides the available objective rules when there is conflicting evidence in children as old as 11 (Shultz and Wells 1985).

Three-year-olds not only can understand the difference between intended and unintended outcomes of actions; they also have some understanding of the moral relevance of intentions (Shultz 1980). For example, if they are given information that the outcome of someone's action was different from what the person intended, they will make use of this in making moral judgements.

Although these studies do establish that children as young as 3 have a concept of intention, just how the concept of intention is related to metarepresentation is not yet understood very well. Astington (in press) has argued that their concept of intention is simply the concept of a desired outcome, and not the concept of intention-as-mental-representation. Evidence for the richer concept of intention, she argues, does not appear until children are about 5.

Some researchers, though, are convinced that children as young as 3 do have virtually the same common-sense psychological framework as adults. Wellman, for example, argues that

> by age 3 children are engaged in the same folk-psychological
> enterprise that we as adults are – understanding human
> behaviour via the internal mental states of the actor, that is, via
> his or her beliefs, desires and intentions. Specifically, while
> 3-year-olds' understanding of human action may not always or
> largely be accurate with respect to a comprehensive folk
> psychological framework for action, it is nonetheless sensible
> with respect to that framework. Even when wrong, young
> people are in the same theoretical ballpark.
>
> (Wellman 1988: 80)

He bases his claim on recent experimental studies (Wellman and Bartsch, in press), and on naturalistic studies of a single child within one month of its third birthday (Shatz, Wellman, and Silber 1983; Wellman 1985). In the former, subjects as young as 3 were able to predict where another would look for a lost puppy when the subjects were told (a) that the other wants to find the puppy, (b) where the puppy is hiding, and (c) where the other thinks the puppy is hiding. In the latter, the child actually engaged in psychological-explanatory conversations. Here is one sample:

> Mom: Don't touch this cloth when your hands are dirty.
> Child: Do my hands look like they're dirty?
> Mom: Yes, they look very dirty.
> Child: Why I painted on them?
> Mom: Why did you?
> Child: Because I thoughted my hands are paper!

Wellman concludes from these studies that 'it would be impossible for children and adults to engage in such conversations at all unless they shared a common folk psychological framework for interpreting behaviour' (1988: 83). As we shall soon see, however, 3-year-olds still lack three of the crucial cognitive abilities underlying common sense that were discussed in Chapter 2. So perhaps Wellman's characterization of them as sharing our basic folk-psychological framework is too generous.

Not only is rational psychology beginning to make its appearance in the descriptions and explanations of behaviour provided by two- and three-year-old children, they are also beginning to put together a realist view of the world and their own relation to its ingredients. During this period children first show that they have a limited ability to recognize representational diversity, in that they realize that another person may perceive, know, want, or like something that they do not, and vice versa (Flavell 1988). Children between 2½ and 3 are capable of thinking about other people's mental processes, they appear to have a rudimentary theory of perception based on perceptibility (Yaniv and Shatz 1988), and they know that one can perceive an object by one sense modality when one cannot perceive it by another. For example, one can sometimes hear something that one cannot at that moment see (Flavell, Green, and Flavell, unpublished manuscript). Flavell and his colleagues have found that children of this age implicitly understand, as shown by their behaviour in experimental situations, that in order for another person to see an object, at least one of the person's eyes must be open and aimed in the general direction of the object, there must not be any occluding object on the line of sight between the person and the object, and what one sees oneself or does not see regarding the other, the object, or any interposed object has no bearing on what the other sees (Flavell 1988; Flavell 1978; Lempers, Flavell, and Flavell 1977).

By the age of 3, children spontaneously begin to make a verbal contast between real things and imaginary or other 'unreal' things such as dreamed-of objects, which are merely mentally represented and have no independent, extramental existence (Shatz, Wellman, and Silber 1983). By the time they are 3, they can give a systematic account of this distinction, as Wellman and his colleagues have shown in a series of experiments (Wellman 1985, 1988; Wellman and Estes 1986). They distinguish between real things and dream entities, imagined entities, and pretend entities in terms of three criteria: (a) real entities, but not merely mental entities, can be perceived and manipulated (you can see them and play with them); (b) they are publicly perceivable, and (c) they have a consistent existence over time (they are there even when you're not thinking about them).

There is even evidence that children as young as 3 have an understanding of what it is for an external object or array to represent a situation. In a study by deLoache (1987), children were given the task of locating an object hidden under some furniture. They were shown a three-dimensional model of the room, in which a model of the object was shown under a model of the furniture. Children aged 3 and older succeeded at the task, but younger children could make no use of the model in performing the task. However, this result does not indicate that children of 3 have any understanding of mental (internal) representation, as opposed to pictorial (external) representation. The latter, after all, is a common feature of their environment, and is made salient to them by means of children's picture books and other symbolic media. In fact, the onset of pretence can usefully be interpreted as the beginning of the child's recognition of symbols: things that can be used to stand for, refer to, that is, represent other things or situations (Olson, unpublished manuscript).

The metarepresentational capacities of young children also can be inferred by studying their behaviour during 'replica' play: play with figures representing people, animals, and things. Wolf, Rygh, and Altshuler (1984) have traced three stages of development, from the prelinguistic infant to the 4-year-old.

> In a first phase, children exhibit implicit understanding of agency and experience in themselves and others. With the onset of symbolic capacities, both of these concepts can be made explicit through language, gesture and their combined use in play. During this second phase, children first represent the agency of different actors. Subsequently, they begin to represent, explain, and reflect on internal experiences as a part of the human repertoire. The data from replica play discussed

here demonstrate that, by age four years, even in the hypothetical situations of replica play, the children we studied were able to attribute sensations, perceptions, emotions, obligations, and cognitions to figures.

(Wolf *et al.*1984: 208)

Three to five: the watershed

Appearance-reality

As impressive as the metarepresentational accomplishments of 3-year-olds are, however, they are still severely limited in comparison with 4- and 5-year-olds. In fact, a major developmental threshold seems to be passed by most children some time between the ages of 4 and 5. This shows up very clearly in regard to their ability to make appearance–reality distinctions. As Flavell and his colleagues have demonstrated in a number of important studies, 3-year-olds have little or no grasp of this distinction. They do poorly on even the easiest experimental tasks, and do not improve as a result of training or by being given clues designed to make the distinction salient to them. When first shown a sponge cleverly painted to resemble a rock and then allowed to handle it, children of this age will say that it both is a sponge and looks like a sponge (the 'intellectual-realism' error). Alternatively, if they are shown a white card and then see the experimenter place a blue transparent film over it, they say that the card both looks blue and is blue (the 'phenomenism' error) (Flavell 1986). They will persist in saying this even if a small, white portion of the card is allowed to project beyond the edge of the blue film (Flavell 1986). Whether they make the phenomenism error or the intellectual-realism error depends upon the type of task, but within tasks they are consistent: they give the same answer to the 'appearance' and the 'reality' questions. Children 3 years of age and younger, therefore, and not adults, appear to be the true 'naïve realists'. It is they who systematically mistake appearance for reality, and vice versa.

These appearance–reality difficulties are displayed over a wide variety of tasks. Three-year-olds have trouble with the distinction between an object's real and apparent identity, colour, shape, size, and number (Flavell 1986, 1988; Flavell, Green, and Flavell 1986). Children of the same age from different cultures perform badly on the same tasks. Flavell *et al.* (1983) found that Chinese and American 3-year-olds have the same difficulties with real vs.

apparent colour, size, and object identity. Attempts to teach children of this age the appearance–reality distinction in the case of real vs. apparent size (Braine and Shanks 1965) and real vs. apparent colour (Flavell, Green, and Flavell 1986) have been unsuccessful.

In sharp contrast with the 3-year-olds, most 5-year-old children have little difficulty with the same appearance–reality tasks that stump the younger children. Although they continue to have difficulty throughout childhood in reflecting on and talking about distinctions couched in terminology such as 'looks different from the way it really and truly is' (Flavell 1986), their performance of tasks requiring them to make these distinctions in practice is quite good (Flavell 1986, 1988).

There is also evidence that the ability to distinguish between someone's real and apparent emotional state develops at approximately the same age, though it is likely that the perceptual appearance–reality distinction is mastered first. Harris (Harris and Gross 1988), for example, found that a minority of 4-year-olds, but nearly all 6-year-olds could readily distinguish between a story character's real emotion and a feigned emotion when they are given information about the event that produces the emotion and also a reason that the person would have for concealing it. Here is one of their stories.

> Diana is playing a game with a friend. At the end of the game
> Diana wins and her friend loses. Diana tries to hide how she
> feels because otherwise her friend won't play anymore.
>
> (Harris and Gross 1988: 296)

Again, there seem to be no effects of cultural difference. Harris (Harris, Donnelly, Guz, and Pitt-Watson 1986; Harris, Gardner, and Gross 1987; Gardner, Harris, Ohmoto, and Hamazaki, in press) found no difference in the performance of 4- and 6-year-olds from Great Britain, the USA, and Japan on these tasks, even though these cultures differ in their social conventions concerning the acceptability of displaying one's emotions at an early age.

The persistence of these difficulties, and their independence of culture, leads Flavell and others to conclude that 3-year-olds' difficulties with the appearance–reality distinction are 'non-trivial, deep-seated and intellectual' (Flavell 1988).

Representational diversity

The experimental evidence suggests that there is also a

developmental breakthrough in understanding representational diversity, which takes place at about the same age of 4 to 5. As reported above, children as young as 2 and 3 understand that another may not see something that one sees oneself; but by the age of 4 to 5, they have acquired the understanding that something that is seen by both oneself and another may look differently or give rise to different experiences if viewed from different positions. For example, 3- and 4-year-old children were shown a picture of a turtle horizontally displayed on a sheet of transparent glass and were asked whether it would look right side up, or vice versa, to an observer seated on the opposite side of the glass. Whereas all children understood the question, the 3-year-olds seemed not to comprehend that the turtle could look one way to them and another way to the observer; but the 4-year-olds had no difficulty answering the question correctly (Masangkay *et al.* 1974; Flavell *et al.* 1980; Flavell *et al.* 1981). Similarly, 4-year-olds performed much better than 3-year-olds in tasks in which they had to attend to and reason about projective size and shape. The older children, for instance, could predict that an object about to be moved away from the subject and towards the experimenter would look smaller to the subject and larger to the experimenter (Pillow and Flavell 1986).

Several studies have shown that at about age 4, but *not* at age 3, children can recognize the difference in people's knowledge of a situation based on differences in the availability of a particular mode of perceptual experience. For example, Maratsos (1973) found that children of this age adjust their speech when giving descriptions of objects to others who are blindfolded; Mossler, Marvin, and Greenberg (1976) found that 4-year-olds realize that those who watch a video presentation with the sound turned off don't have the same information as those who both see and hear the presentation; and Marvin, Greenberg, and Mossler (1976) showed that 4-year-olds can identify who has learned a secret depending on who whispered to whom or whose eyes were covered.

Gopnik and Graf (1988), in an experiment with children of 3 and 4, allowed some children to look inside a box to see the toy inside, whereas others were told what was inside, and still others were presented with clues that allowed them to infer what was inside the box. They found that the 3-year-old children could correctly report what was in the box, but they were unable to identify the source of their knowledge. The 4-year-olds, though, had no trouble reporting both the identity of the object in the box and also how they came to know it.

Turkish is a language in which the evidential source for an assertion is marked syntactically, depending upon whether the reported situation was actually perceived, or was inferred, or told to one by another. Turkish children begin to make use of this syntactical device as early as 4 to 4½ (Aksu-Koc and Slobin 1986).

One important indication of the ability to understand representational diversity is the ability to recognize that others may have false beliefs about things that one knows oneself. The ability to attribute false beliefs has been extensively studied by Wimmer and Perner and their associates in a number of well-known experiments (Wimmer and Perner 1983; Perner, Leekam, and Wimmer 1987; Wimmer, Hogrefe, and Sodian 1988). In one experiment, children watch a puppet show in which a puppet witnesses a piece of chocolate being placed in a drawer of a cabinet. The puppet then leaves the room, and during its absence, but in full view of the child, the chocolate is taken out of the original drawer and placed in another. The child is then told that the puppet will want to get some chocolate when it returns, and is asked where it will look for the chocolate. In order to answer the question correctly, the child must represent the chocolate as being in the second drawer, while simultaneously representing the puppet as believing that the chocolate is in the first drawer. Three-year-old children consistently predict that the puppet will look in the second drawer (i.e., where the chocolate actually is), but 4-year-olds overwhelmingly predict that it will look in the first drawer. Note that neither the correct prediction of the 4-year-olds nor the incorrect prediction of the 3-year-olds would be intelligible unless each child also believed that the absent puppet will want to find the chocolate. Our ability to label action predictions as correct or incorrect depends on our assuming that the people's action predictions will fit the pattern of rational psychology.

Children of 3 are able to attribute ignorance to others (Hogrefe, Wimmer, and Perner 1986), so they understand that another may not know where the chocolate is; but they evidently do not understand that another can have a false belief on a matter about which one has knowledge oneself. That is, they do not understand that another can have a positive mental representation of a situation that is different from, and incompatible with, what oneself knows to be the case (Flavell 1988). The failure of the 3-year-olds on the false-belief task is not attributable to their failure to remember where the chocolate originally was placed or to remember that the puppet did not witness it being moved (Wimmer and Perner 1983); nor does making explicit for them the expectations giving rise to the false belief assist them to infer it in others, even in real-life situations in which they are trapped into having false beliefs themselves, based on those very expectations (Perner, Leekam, and Wimmer 1987).

One of the most important implications of the difference in performance between 3-year-olds and 4-year-olds on false-belief tasks is that only the older children are rational psychologists in the same way that adults are. The older children explain people's actions by appealing to their representational states: their desiderative states and their epistemic states. People act as they do because of what they desire and what they believe. But the younger children think that people's actions are a function of people's desires and the way the world actually is. They think that a person who wants a piece of candy will look in the drawer where the candy actually is. It is not until they have recognized the facts of representational diversity, especially as shown in the false-belief cases, that they will come to realize that a person who wants a piece of candy will look where the person believes the candy is, whether or not it is actually there. If this is so, then it will be necessary to modify Wellman's (1988) claim that 'by age 3 children are engaged in the same folk-psychological enterprise that we as adults are – understanding human behaviour via the internal mental states of the actor, that is, via his or her beliefs, desires and intentions'.

One would expect that children who cannot predict the false beliefs of others would fare very badly in situations in which a premium is put on the ability to deceive others and to recognize deceptive attempts on the part of others, for deception requires the ability to estimate what another is likely to believe given certain conditions. It also involves the ability to estimate what the other will think one believes oneself, and the ability to recognize another as being aware of one's own intentions. Shultz found that this 'recursive' awareness of intention is present in 5-year-olds, but has not yet appeared in 3-year-olds (Shultz 1980; Shultz and Cloghesy 1981). Harris and Gross (1988) point out that the ability to distinguish between real and apparent emotion, which develops between the ages of 4 and 6, depends upon understanding that people's facial expressions can be simulated specifically in order to deceive an observer. A typical childhood situation in which recursive reasoning is required is a strategic game such as hide-and-seek, which children are unable to play with any success before the age of 4 or 5 (Gratch 1964; DeVries 1970; Shultz and Cloghesy 1981). La Frenière (1988) has also found that children younger than about 5 are unable to devise effective strategies for deceiving others in strategic games of the sort in which an opponent has to guess whether one has hidden some object (for example, a toy bear) inside a toy house, or in a toy tower, or in a trunk.

Representational change

Most significantly, the development of the ability to make the appearance–reality distinction and the ability to recognize representational diversity are highly correlated with each other; children who are successful at appearance–reality tasks are successful at representational diversity tasks, and those who do poorly in appearance–reality tasks also do poorly in representational diversity tasks (Gopnik and Astington 1988). These two abilities are also correlated with the development of the ability to recognize representational change, as Gopnik and Astington (1988) found in a number of experiments on 3-, 4-, and 5-year-olds, which were related to the Wimmer and Perner (1983) false-belief paradigm and to the tasks Flavell and his colleagues used to test for the appearance–reality distinction (Astington and Gopnik 1988; Gopnik and Astington 1988). In one experiment, children were shown a book with pictures of familiar animals on the cover (a cat, a rabbit, and so on). The book was then opened to reveal a page with a circular cut-out in the centre, through which part of a figure could be seen. The page was turned to reveal the picture of a rabbit, the ears of which had been visible through the cut-out. The next page also had a cut-out, and when it was turned the following page revealed a dog, the ears of which had been visible through the cut-out on the previous page. When the next page was turned to reveal a cut-out with a figure behind it, many children spontaneously identified the partially hidden figure as a cat; but when the page was turned and the full figure was revealed, it was clearly the picture of a flower, the top two petals of which (resembling a cat's ears and the top of a cat's head) had been visible through the cut-out. Other experiments involved the Flavell sponge-rock, a picture of a red cat covered by a green transparent film, a Smartie box which turned out upon being opened to contain pencil-stubs, and a doll in a dress which turned out on being undressed to be two dolls, one standing on the other's shoulders. In each case children were asked an appearance–reality question, a false-belief question (for example, Nicky hasn't seen this before: will he think that it's a picture of a cat behind this cut-out, or will he think it's a picture of a flower?), and a representational-change question (When you first saw this picture through the cut-out, before I turned the page, did you think it was a cat or a flower?). The 5-year-olds performed well on all questions on all tasks, the 4-year-olds performed fairly well on most of them, but significantly better than the 3-year-olds, who performed poorly on all questions on all tasks. On the representational-change question, for example, most 3-year-olds said that they had thought that it was a flower even before the cut-out page was turned, even though just a few moments before some of the very same children had spontaneously volunteered that it was (going to be) a cat.

Most investigators now agree that something important happens at about the age of 4 in the child's acquisition of the common-sense view of the world. (Indeed, this is the guiding theme explored by the contributors to Astington, Harris, and Olson 1988.) An important watershed in the ability to make metarepresentational distinctions is crossed. For the first time, the child is beginning to make the sorts of second-order distinctions among first-order mental representations characteristic of adults. Johnson and Wellman, for example, have argued that by age 4 children are forming a concept of mind, in that they do not merely refer to individual mental phenomena using the 'mentalistic' vocabulary they have acquired; they show that they are able to organize a variety of 'mentalistic' terms under broader categories, indicating that they recognize a category of mental phenomena and mental acts (Johnson and Wellman 1982; Johnson 1982; Wellman 1985, 1988). It is at this age, also, that children begin to attribute sensations, emotions, obligations, and cognitive acts and processes to figures in replica play, thus showing that they have an idea of an agent as guided in behaviour by mental representations (Wolf, Rygh, and Altshuler 1984).

There is less widespread agreement about what underlying developmental factor underlies the virtually simultaneous appearance of the ability to make appearance–reality distinctions, the ability to recognize representational change, and the ability to acknowledge representational diversity. It is to competing accounts of the 4-year-old watershed that we must now turn.

4

The origins of common sense: the representational model of the mind

Most researchers agree that there is a significant breakthrough in the child's cognitive development at about age 4, with the onset of, first, the ability to make reliable appearance–reality distinctions, second, the cognizance of the various types of representational diversity (perceptual perspective-taking, conceptual perspective-taking, attribution of false beliefs), and third, the recognition of representational change, though there are some who disagree with the view that the 4-year-old achievements constitute an important developmental threshold (for example, Chandler 1988). Although there are still significant cognitive developments to come, of course, the way 4- to 5-year-old children conceive of the relation between perceivers, thinkers, and agents and the world they perceive, think about, and act within and upon, is much closer to the adult common-sense view than that of 2- and 3-year-olds, not to mention infants. Yet there is far less agreement on precisely how to characterize the underlying cognitive development that explains the appearance of these three crucial cognitive abilities at this period. What underlying capacity has the 4-year-old acquired which enables her to make adult-like distinctions that are completely beyond her only slightly younger siblings?

Since each of the abilities appearing at approximately age 4 requires the capacity to form second-order representations of first-order mental representations, perhaps we need look no further than the development of the metarepresentational ability for an answer to our question. If you can't represent yourself and others as having mental representations, then you can't recognize that something can appear to you to be other than it really is, or that it can present a different appearance to someone else from the way it looks to you; nor can you make sense of the idea that someone else can believe the world to be different from the way you know it to be; nor can you recognize that a few moments ago you believed the world to be one way, whereas now you know it to be a different way. This is true enough; but it doesn't follow from this, of course, that if one can metarepresent one can also make these other distinctions. And in fact, we have seen evidence that children begin to metarepresent between the ages of 18 months and 2 years, when they first begin to engage in pretence, recognize others as engaging in pretence, and make reference in their conversations to a variety of their own and others' representational states. As Leslie (1988) puts it, why do they have to wait half a lifetime to acquire the additional meta-representational abilities of recognizing false belief, and so on?

Leslie's (1987, 1988) own explanation for this long developmental delay is that the 2- and 3-year-olds haven't yet understood the complex way in which mental representations function causally. They have learned to 'decouple', or detach, the representational contents of their primary mental representations from their normal reference and their normal 'input and output relations' (namely, being caused by perception of the environment and causing environmentally appropriate behaviour). So they can suspend, or 'bracket', the belief that this perceived thing is a banana, they can temporarily assign it a deviant reference (for example, telephone), and they can behave towards and with it in a way rather like, but not exactly like, that which would normally be appropriate to a telephone. What would otherwise be a 'transparent' mental representation, in which the child is unaware of the representation as representation but automatically 'refers' it to the world, now becomes 'opaque': the child is now aware of it as a representation, or as Olson (unpublished) says, a symbol, which may be used by the child to have any reference she chooses. The normal inferential relations, truth conditions, and so on, appropriate to it as a representation of a banana (for example, is a piece of fruit, is sweet-tasting, and so on) are suspended for the duration of the pretence, even though the child still believes what she sees is a banana, at the same time that she is pretending that it is (i.e., is representing it as) a telephone.

But young metarepresenters, according to Leslie, do not yet understand 'the way in which mental states are part of the causal fabric of the world' (1987: 27). As Wellman (1985, 1988) has shown, by the time they are 3, children are aware that one cannot actually see or act on imaginary or dream objects, and they realize that they are not publicly observable. 'They understand that bananas may be eaten but thoughts about bananas may not. Thus, the three-year-old already thinks of mental states as *"immaterial" and abstract* entities' (Leslie 1987: 27). But they have yet to understand how mental states are caused. In particular, they are not aware of how beliefs arise, and hence how false beliefs arise. They make use of their metarepresentational capacity to generate metarepresentations, in pretence and in attribution of mental states to others. But 'it may not occur to the three-year-old that mental states are actually caused by things – by concrete events – and that they are, in turn, the causes of other concrete things – behaviour' (1988: 35). The developmental step that is required before the child can recognize false belief, and presumably other varieties of representational diversity and the appearance–reality distinction, is 'the ability to think of mental states as abstract entities which nevertheless have concrete causes and concrete effects' (1987: 28), a step which may be all the more difficult, Leslie thinks, precisely because they think of mental states as immaterial and abstract, and hence have difficulty placing them within a causal network.

Leslie's account, then, is that the young children lack a particular sort of information, causal information, to enable them to apply their metarepresentational abilities to tasks requiring an understanding of the causal continuity of mental states with the physical world. Leslie's 2- and 3-year-olds are dualists: they recognize the difference between concrete, material entities and abstract, immaterial entities.[1] But they are not yet Cartesian interactive dualists: they haven't yet recognized that mental representations can causally interact with the physical world.

If this is supposed to have the consequence that 3-year-olds do not recognize psychological causality, however, Leslie is just wrong. As Hood and Bloom (1979) point out, children of 2 to 3 years of age seem much more aware of psychological causality than of physical causality; they know that things in the world cause emotional states and desires, for example, and they know that intentions, desires, and beliefs are causal determinants of action (Wellman 1988). These are examples of attributing mental representations as causes and effects of concrete situations in the world. So it doesn't seem that ignorance of the fact that mental representations are part of the causal fabric of the world is going to explain the two-year developmental lag.

I have difficulties with Leslie's causal hypothesis on other grounds as well. Three-year-olds may not yet understand how beliefs are caused, as Leslie says; but that may be because they haven't yet acquired the concept of a belief as a mental representation with a truth-value: i.e., which may or may not be true; and not because they haven't yet understood that immaterial entities can have material causes and effects. If this is the case, it may be because they haven't yet understood that actual, real-world states of affairs are mentally represented as well as imaginary, dreamed-of, or merely thought-about states of affairs. One can have the conception of an imaginary object as an 'immaterial entity' without having the conception of a belief as an immaterial state, or of a perceptual experience, for example the way something looks (is represented) from here, as in any way immaterial. If one doesn't yet have the concept of a belief as a representational state, then of course one will not have an understanding of its causal sources and products. The alleged immateriality-but-causal-efficacy of mental representations is, in my view, a red herring

Wimmer, Hogrefe, and Sodian (1988) have offered an explanation of the cognitive achievements of 4-year-olds in comparison with 3-year-olds which, like Leslie's account, also appeals to a deficiency in causal understanding. According to their account, the younger children lack an understanding of how they know something or have come to have a true or false belief. They are ignorant of whether their access to the information was via perception of the situation itself, was the result of verbal communication from another, or was the consequence of an inference from available evidence. They have

> not yet conceptualized the most basic informational conditions like perception and communication as origins of knowledge and belief in human minds... [Thus they] do not understand why or how they know something, or why they were trapped into a false belief... [and] they do not understand what another person knows or believes when only the informational sources of the other person are available to them.
>
> (Wimmer, Hogrefe, and Sodian 1988: 173–4)

The breakthrough comes when they begin to 'relate such informational conditions as seeing or hearing in an explicit way to their already existing conceptions of knowledge and belief, and thus they become aware of these informational conditions as causal origins of knowledge and belief' (1988: 174). But the accomplishments of the 4-year-old are only partial. Because they now have an understanding of perception and verbal communication as information sources, they can recognize some forms of representational diversity (for example, false belief, the standard perceptual perspective-taking tasks), and they have acquired facility in making appearance–reality distinctions. But until they are about 6, they ignore other 'informational access' determinants of mental representations, such as inference and the quality of verbal information. Four-year-olds still seem to think that if someone else has seen something or has received any sort of message about it, it will be known by them. They are still unable to recognize that the other may not have seen an identifying feature of the object (poor quality of perceptual information), or that the message may have been ambiguous, and hence insufficient to allow identification from the message content alone (poor quality of verbal information). They are unable to follow the 'deficit check' strategy of checking the informational source to determine whether it provides sufficient information to provide the other with the knowledge one has oneself.

Forguson and Gopnik. Quite a different sort of account of the underlying cognitive development explaining the achievements of the 4-year-old has been advanced by Forguson and Gopnik (1988). Rather than appealing to a 'quantitative' improvement in the child's information about the causal factors affecting belief and knowledge, they argue that the 4-year-old's achievement represents a 'qualitative', conceptual breakthrough in understanding the mediating role of the mind in all perception and thought.

The metarepresentational achievements of children aged 3 years and younger can be seen as falling into two broad categories. First, they recognize that they and others can represent objects and situations that are not currently perceived. People remember incidents in the past; they anticipate, desire, plan for, and intend to accomplish situations in the future; they hypothesize about what situation would or might exist if... Second, they understand that people represent in thought 'fictive' things and situations. People imagine monsters; they dream of bizarre situations; they pretend that the empty cup has tea in it. These categories of objects of mental representation are both composed of things and situations which, in some sense, do not exist, or at least do not currently exist, except in so far as they are subjectively represented. The past is gone; the future has not yet begun; desires may never be satisfied; intentions may not be fulfilled. And we have seen that 3-year-olds understand that imaginary and dream objects, and the pretend-tea in the real cup, cannot be publicly observed and are not really perceived by oneself (Wellman 1988). They are not objective features of the world, and no one is aware of them but oneself (unless one tells someone else). For the 3-year-old, one mentally represents what one cannot perceive. These mentally represented situations have an 'inner' source, even if they are not under voluntary control. It doesn't occur to them that one also mentally represents something if it's actually being perceived, or if it's an existing, current situation that one is thinking about.

Forguson and Gopnik point out that success in the appearance–reality, representational-diversity, and representational-change tasks is contingent upon the child being able to recognize and make effective use of the fact that *real* things and situations that one is currently perceiving or thinking about are also mentally represented, and hence that people's mental representations can vary independently of the real nature of the situation being represented. Three-year-olds also have some understanding of the conditions of perceptibility (Yaniv and Shatz 1988), and they recognize that another may perceive (or fail to perceive) some object or situation that one does not (or does) oneself. But they do not realize that a situation that is perceived both by oneself and by another may be interpreted differently by the two perceivers; nor do they realize that people may have different, and incompatible, beliefs about the same situation. The deficit in both of these cases is the same: they fail to understand that *actual* objects and situations, even currently perceived ones, are mentally represented. In thinking about other people's cognitive successes and failures, they metarepresent what are in fact other people's mental representations, but the 3-year-olds do not represent them *as* representations, whereas the 4-year-olds do.2

They realize that not only are we in perceptual and cognitive contact with things in the world outside our skins, but also that to be in such contact requires mentally representing it in some way. To see *X*, *X* must look some way or other to one (seeing is always seeing *as*); to hear something, it must sound some way or other to one, and so on for the other sensory modalities: to perceive something bymodality *M* is necessarily to mentally represent it modulo-*M* as.... Likewise, to remember some event in the past (i.e., the episodic memory of one's own past experiences, and not merely the semantic memory of facts) is to mentally represent that past situation in one's present consciousness. To anticipate something one thinks is going to happen ('it's real, it just hasn't happened yet') is to mentally represent it. Once one realizes that the mind is a 'representational organ', that cognitive contact with the real world as well as the 'mere' representation of the dream world, and so on, is a matter of mental representation, one is in the cognitive position to compare and contrast any sort of mental representation with any other, and make epistemic use of this information. There is still a contrast between the real and the merely imagined, merely dreamed-about, and this is the contrast even the 3-year-olds have mastered (Wellman 1988), but it is no longer construed as a contrast between the real (and therefore unrepresented) and the (merely) represented.

The cognitive achievement of the 4-year-olds is characterized by Forguson and Gopnik as the acquisition of a representational model of the mind. The 3-year-olds' view of cognition was dichotomous: one either has direct and unmediated contact with real, currently existing things and situations, in which case everyone who has any information about them has the same information; or one mentally represents 'unreal', or at least not currently real, things and situations, regarding which people's mental states differ. But the older children have forged a more unified view of the mind as a 'representational organ': perception, belief, imagination, dreaming, pretending, all involve mental representation, whether the origin of the representation is in oneself or in the world. The world that we perceptually experience and think about is independent of our thought and experience; but it is represented in thought and experience. To think about or perceive is always to mentally represent, even if the content of one's experience or thought does not always constitute accurate information about the way the world actually is.

A representational model of the mind doesn't distinguish between 'mere' mental representations on the one hand, and direct perceptual and cognitive contact with the real world on the other. Rather, it involves adopting the metacognitive view that some of one's mental representations

> are one's own personal viewpoint on a reality independent of this or any other private, personal viewpoint; that they are effects in oneself caused by the action of that independent reality on one's senses; that representations provide information about the way reality stands; that different people have a different informational relation to reality than oneself; that one's own informational relation to reality changes constantly.
>
> (Forguson and Gopnik 1988: 236)

Other representations, however, have their origins not in the 'outer' world but in oneself. But all mental representations, however caused, can themselves have effects in the world via one's own behaviour.

One could not recognize that mental representations are 'part of the causal fabric of the world' (Leslie 1988), nor that different conditions and forms of informational access give rise to different mental representations (Wimmer, Hogrefe, and Sodian 1988), unless one has acquired a representational model of the mind, according to which all of one's knowledge and beliefs about actual things and situations in the world are mediated by mental representations. The causal explanations of Leslie and of Wimmer *et al.* thus presuppose the sort of metacognitive viewpoint that Forguson and Gopnik propose.

In addition, as Astington and Gopnik (1988) have argued, although the appearance–reality and representational-diversity data are amenable to a causal explanation, according to which the 3-year-olds are deficient in causal knowledge that 4-year-olds have, the same cannot be said for the representational-change data. Here, it is irrelevant how one has come to have one's new belief, or how one came to have one's old one. The crucial fact is merely that the belief has changed: one used to represent the box as having Smarties in it; one now represents it as having pencils in it. The 'qualitative change' account of Forguson and Gopnik accounts for this result quite nicely. For the 3-year-old, either you know something via direct cognitive contact, or you are ignorant of it. To recognize that you used to think the box had Smarties in it but now know that there are pencils in it requires the ability to entertain two representations simultaneously, marking one as one's present correct representation (knowledge) and the other as one's former representation (false belief). But it is not required that one represent, or be in any way cognizant of, how one's representation of the situation came to change.

To say that 4-year-old children have developed a representational model of the mind does not, of course, imply that they have any conception of the specific mechanisms of mental representation. They do not have any idea about how the mind represents things and situations. They have a basic conception of the mind's function, but not of how it carries out that function. Indeed, apart from theoretically minded psychologists and philosophers, even most adults have no views on this matter. Theories such as Fodor's (1987) representational theory of the mind attempt to answer the question as to how it is possible for the mind to represent actual and counterfactual things and states of affairs. Four-year-old children do not have any such theory, not even a primitive version of it. But they do have the main features of what I have called a *theorette*. They make ontological distinctions which play an essential role in unified, law-like explanation of perception, thought, and action.

Flavell (1988) offers a somewhat similar account of the difference between the cognitive abilities of 2- and 3-year-olds and those of 4- and 5-year olds. In earlier works (for example, Flavell 1986), he made descriptive categorization of the younger children's, cognitive abilities across a number of domains in comparison with those of the older pre-school children. His studies focused especially on the appearance–reality distinction and two categories of representational diversity: perceptual perspective-taking and conceptual perspective-taking. The younger children he called 'level 1' children; the older ones were categorized as 'level 2' children. His new account attempts to pinpoint the underlying cognitive capacities that are characteristic of these two developmental stages.

Level 1 children have a basic understanding that they and others have 'cognitive connections' with things in the world by means of perception and thought. They also have, as we have seen earlier in the present chapter, some understanding: (a) that the cognitive connections they have with things can change over time; (b) that they are for the most part independent of one another; (c) that their own cognitive connections to things are independent of the cognitive connections other people have with things; (d) that cognitive connections involve inner, subjective experiences. They also believe that objects and events in the world 'have a single nature', in that there is a single way that each thing or event actually *is* (where 'the way *X* is' is not differentiated by them from 'the way *X* seems to me at the moment'): it cannot really be two different ways simultaneously. But level 1 children

> tend not to understand that forming cognitive connections to things entails mentally representing those things in various ways. They tend to be largely ignorant of the fact that it is possible to represent a single nature in several different ways ...
> Thus, they do not clearly understand that even though something may be only one way out there in the world, it can be more than one way up here in our heads, in our mental representations of it.
>
> (Flavell 1988: 246)

It is precisely this additional representational ability that distinguishes level 2 children from level 1 children. In order to accomplish the appearance–reality tasks and the various representational-diversity tasks, not to speak of the representational-change tasks, they must somehow recognize, if only implicitly, that to be cognitively connected with some feature of the world is to mentally represent it. Having realized that, they are in a position to understand that representations of a single reality can vary even though the represented world does not. As Russell (1988) puts it, they are in a position to realize that there is an asymmetry between representations and situations represented. They are also then in a position to understand that not only do mental representations differ among people, or within the same person at different times; they can lead to mistakes, such as false beliefs generally and perceptual illusions in particular. Anyone whose cognitive contact with reality is mediated by representations is also a potential, and perhaps not all that infrequent, mis-representer.

Unlike the developmental accounts of Leslie, and of Wimmer, Hogrefe, and Sodian, where the difference between the level 1 and the level 2 children is essentially quantitative (i.e., they don't have enough information about causal relations), Flavell, like Forguson and Gopnik, thinks that the deficiencies of the level 1 children are qualitative: they are, in his words, 'non-trivial, deep-seated and intellectual' (1988: 249). The level 2 children have, and the level 1 children lack, a certain kind of understanding. And it is an understanding that is best expressed by saying that the level 2 children have a certain kind of understanding about mental representations that the level 1 children lack.

Although I am in agreement with Flavell's identification of the development of an understanding about mental representation as the key to the breakthrough on the part of the level 2 children, I do not think that his contrast between knowledge of cognitive connections and knowledge of mental representations adequately captures the qualitative difference between the level 1 and the level 2 children. This can be seen by focusing on a conceptual–logical confusion embedded in Flavell's characterization of the level 1 children's cognitive stage. To be cognitively connected with something is to be related to it in a certain way. To be cognitively connected with a banana via visual perception is for the asymmetrical relation '… sees …' to obtain between the perceiver and the banana. That is what is involved in taking the idea of connection seriously in the expression 'cognitive connection'. But relations presuppose relata. For the relation 'S sees X' to obtain, both S and X must actually exist. Now everything we perceive does, of course, actually exist. So the level 1 child's understanding of perception can without distortion be expressed by saying that it is an understanding of the fact that people can be cognitively connected with things in the world via perception. But not all objects of thought are things in the world. Imaginary objects aren't, nor are the objects in dreams, to mention just two examples. So we cannot really be cognitively connected to these objects by means of imagination and dreaming (which Flavell, along with Descartes, presumably would classify as 'modes of thought'). This, after all, is one of the ontological aspects of the problem of intentionality. How can it be true of me that I am thinking about a unicorn if there are no unicorns? Well, I cannot be cognitively connected with a unicorn, but I can be cognitively connected with a mental representation of a unicorn, a 'unicorn-representation', to use Nelson Goodman's (1968) terminology, so that we acknowledge that no actual relation exists between me and a unicorn when I represent a unicorn.

As we have seen, 3-year-old children do understand the difference between things in the world, which can be perceived by themselves and others, and which exist even when they and others are not perceiving them, and unreal things which lack these characteristics. The latter are, we might say, mere representations. But then, the level 1 child must after all have a concept of mental representation. If the level 1 child's understanding of the distinction between things in the world and mere representations is to be captured within the 'cognitive connections' framework of categorization, then it must be allowed that level 1 children understand that people can form mental representations of things. If not, then the cognitive capacities of the level 1 child cannot be characterized in terms of the distinction between understanding cognitive connections and understanding mental representations.

If the level 1 children do have some understanding of mental representations, though, what is their specific qualitative deficit in relation to level 2 children? It must have to do with the fact that level 2 children understand, whereas level 1 children do not, that our cognitive contact with real things in the world, via perception of and thought about them, is also accomplished by means of mental representations. It is not just 'unreal' things and situations that we mentally represent; all cognitive contact involves mental representation. Much of what Flavell says is similar to, and complementary to, the theory advanced by Forguson and Gopnik; however, his formulation of the 'cognitive contact vs. mental representations' dichotomy does not, and cannot, adequately capture the key to the qualitative deficit of the level 1 children.

Josef Perner's (1988a) account is similar to that of Flavell and of Forguson and Gopnik, in that he is convinced that the cognitive development exhibited by the achievements of the 4-year-olds is a qualitative, conceptual breakthrough in their representational capacity. But he differs from Flavell, from Forguson and Gopnik, and even from Leslie in denying that 2- and 3-year-old children really have the capacity to metarepresent.

Using the concepts and terminology of model-theoretic semantics, Perner construes mental representations as mental models of situations, consisting of elements (for example, objects) and relations (for example, predicates), which can be combined in various ways. If each element in the model is assigned an element in the world as its interpretation, the model becomes a model of the world, which may then be evaluated (as true or false, correct or incorrect) by comparison with that situation. Mental representations are models, on this view, in the same way that sentences are models.

Perner's developmental account has three stages. In the first stage, encompassing the first year or so of life, the infant constructs mental models, but these are entirely determined by perceptual input, and the fact that these models do have the function of representing the world (i.e., that we observers or theorists can understand them as having this role) is a function of the causal relations obtaining between the child's perceptual equipment and the world. The infant's model thus constitutes reality for the infant; it is the infant's 'knowledge base'. It is only from the point of view of the external observer-theorist that the model is interpreted as representing reality.

The second stage is entered when the child acquires the ability to manipulate mental models: to 'transport the mental elements of his knowledge base into another model where he can rearrange these elements in different ways' (1988a: 146). Such a development in representational capacity is presupposed by the child's emerging ability to understand, evaluate, and produce symbolic information such as language and pictures. It also underlies the essentially symbolic activity of pretence. At this stage of development, then, mental models are for the first time used as models by the child: they are interpreted as referring to the real world or to some alternative, pretend, or imaginary world; and they are evaluated as true (or correct) or not, by comparison with the model which is the knowledge base. The child at this stage, though able to use models to represent alternative situations, to interpret them and to evaluate them against the knowledge base, is not yet able to model the modelling relation itself, according to Perner. That is, the child has not yet acquired the ability to model the semantic relationship between a model and what it models, and thus children at this stage do not yet recognize mental states as representational states. This stage, reached at about age 4, is the true meta-representational stage.

Three-year-old and younger children are not metarepresenters, says Perner, because they do not represent representational states as representational states. For example, a representation user (stage two child) can evaluate someone else's model as false (that is, she can associate the other with a counterfactual model); but she does not understand that the other evaluates it as true. To do this, she must not only construct a counterfactual model of the situation and associate the other with it; she must construct a model of the other person's modelling process, including the fact that the other interprets the model as referring to the actual world. Only then will the child be in a position to predict how someone with a false belief about an actual situation will act. False-believers act inappropriately in actual situations in which they want to act appropriately. This can be understood only if one realizes that people act not according to situations, but according to their mental representations of them.

> By conceptualizing the mind as a representational medium the child gains a theoretical understanding of how the mind relates to the external world, in particular the role of mental states in acquiring information and in guiding behaviour. For full understanding of knowledge acquisition the child needs meta-representational abilities. For he has to understand how contact with the world (a certain situation) sets the mental model (internal representation) into a corresponding state (same structural combination of elements). Conceptual understanding of this process means the child has to model the process of information contact. He has to build a model of the external situation and another, metarepresentational model of the mental state, which is itself a model of the external situation.
>
> (Perner 1988a: 151)

One problematic aspect of Perner's view is his semantic model-theoretic account of mental representation. A mental representation is a model, for Perner, with some situation in the world as its interpretation. But words are given an interpretation by language-users, and language-users are typically perceptually aware of the features of the world that are assigned as interpretations of expressions in the language. Thus we determine the truth of people's utterances by comparing what they say (their models) with reality (the interpretations). However, mental representations, if they are understood model-theoretically, would have to have 'natural' or 'original' interpretations, which seems to commit one to a strong version of the language-of-thought theory (see Fodor 1975). Model-theoretic mental semantics thus invites the question: how are the interpretations of the elements in mental models assigned?

Furthermore, nothing but confusion results from saying, as

Perner sometimes does, that we compare our representations with their interpretations, or with situations, and also saying, as he does at other times, that we can only compare representations with other representations (see 1988a:146–9, and note 8). An omniscient observer could determine whether the elements of my knowledge base have real world counterparts, and if so, whether they are truly represented by the elements of the knowledge base. But no explanation is provided of how even the hypothesis of an external world can make sense to me if I can never directly inspect reality, but only my own knowledge base.

A further problem with Perner's account arises from the fact that children younger than 4 seem to have an implicit understanding of the representational process itself. In de Loache's (1987) study, for instance, 3-year-old children who were shown a three-dimensional model depicting a target object hidden under a piece of furniture were able to make use of the model to find the hidden target in the experimental task in the actual room. Perner has to admit that these 3-year-olds have an explicit, abstract concept of representation; but, he says, they don't incorporate this concept into their concept of the mind until a year later. If he means by this that 3-year-olds have a concept of external representation of external reality – that objects and situations in the world can be used to represent other objects and situations in the world – but not until 4 do they generalize this concept to encompass internal representation – that mental states represent objects and situations in the world – then he is in agreement with Forguson and Gopnik that the significant developmental achievement of the 4-year-old is the construction of a representational model of the mind. But unlike Forguson and Gopnik, Flavell, Leslie, and most others interested in the cognitive development of children during this period, Perner denies that 3-year-olds are metarepresenters, and here his view seems to fly in the face of the evidence.

Three-year-olds have a concept of internal representation: they are aware that internal states can represent counterfactual objects and situations, as Wellman's (1988) results show. They are aware that both external states and internal states can function representationally (i.e., symbolically). Even 2-year-old pretenders recognize that others engaged in symbolic play with them are pretending as well: namely, that the others are merely representing the banana as a telephone and know full well that it is really a banana. This shows that they are able to represent the representational process. For me to represent a banana as a telephone is a first-order representational achievement; but for me to be able to represent myself as (merely) representing the banana as a telephone, or for me to represent another as merely representing the banana as a telephone is a metarepresentational achievement. Three-year-olds know that pictures and models are external representations; they even know that there is such a thing as internal representation; the only thing they have not realized is that external situations are internally represented too: perception (even veridical perception) and belief (even true belief) are representational processes. But this next step is a giant step, for it requires conceptualizing the relation between the mind and the world in an entirely new way. It requires, in short, that the child adopt a representational model of the mind.

Later developments

The developmental achievements of the 4-year-old, in comparison with only slightly younger children, are impressive. But 4-year-olds are still not adults. Further refinement and consolidation of the common-sense view continues to take place throughout the primary-school years and even into adolescence. Until the early school years, for example, children continue to have difficulty in recognizing the trouble they and others can have in dealing with ambiguous information. Sodian (1988) found that 4-year-olds who themselves know the location of a hidden object tend to judge that another person who has received an ambiguous message about the location of the object will know where the object is; but by the age of 6, children correctly judge that someone who has received an ambiguous message will be ignorant of the critical fact. Robinson and Robinson (1982) found that 5-year-olds cannot recognize that an ambiguous message gives them insufficient information to identify something via the message, whereas 7-year-olds are proficient at recognizing that ambiguous messages provide insufficient information. They argue that the younger children's failure to recognize ambiguous messages is part of a more general inability to realize when one has insufficient information to interpret correctly what the world is like. Beal and Flavell (1984) found that first-graders (aged 6 and 7) who already know what a speaker's intention is still cannot detect the ambiguity of the speaker's message, whereas if they do not know the speaker's intention, they are able to detect ambiguity. Second-graders, however, can detect ambiguity in both the 'informed of intention' and 'uninformed of intention' conditions. Olson has argued that the development of the ability to distinguish the meaning of a message from the communication intention of the speaker (or writer) may be linked with the acquisition of literacy, where one must learn to infer what the writer meant from the literal meanings of the words on the page (Olson 1977; Olson and Hildyard 1983).

In analogous non-linguistic tasks, children of 5 and 6 who had seen a picture of an animal (for example, an elephant), and then were shown a small, insignificant portion of the animal picture through a cut-out on a covering page, claimed to know the identity of the animal on the basis of seeing the exposed, but ambiguous, portion; and they further judged that others would know the identity of the animal if shown only the exposed portion. A minority of 6-year-olds mastered the task; but only the 9-year-old group were at ceiling. Virtually all of them correctly judged that they did not know what animal it was, even though they saw a portion of it, and they recognized that others would not know the identity of the animal just from seeing the exposed portion (Olson and Astington 1987). In other experiments, children as young as 7 were able to judge correctly that the other would not be able to identify the animal on the basis of seeing the exposed portion alone (Chandler and Helm 1984; Taylor 1988). This suggests that the ability to realize that one and the same 'stimulus event' is likely to be interpreted by different people in different ways depending on what they already know and believe doesn't develop until the early school years. Perner, however, has argued that experiments by himself and Leekam have shown that this ability is indeed present in children of 4–6 years of age (Leekam and Perner 1987; Perner 1988a).

One thing that is characteristic of 4-year-olds in contrast to 6-year-olds is 'the inference neglect'. The younger children judge that others will know a fact if they have had perceptual or communicative access to it; but they will not bother to determine whether the information available to the other was really informative as to the fact (for example, was the communication ambiguous?), and they will tend to attribute ignorance to another who was in a position to infer the fact even if unable to perceive it (Wimmer, Hogrefe, and Sodian 1988; Sodian 1988). They have not yet mastered the idea that what a person knows depends upon what sort of informational access the person has had: direct-perceptual, communicative, or inferential-perceptual (Wimmer, Hogrefe, and Sodian 1988). Put another way, 4-year-olds still have difficulty understanding in what way people come to have the sorts and quality of knowledge and beliefs they have, if the source of that knowledge is inferential. They have not yet come to conceive of the mind as a central processor, which not only receives information from the external world, but also interprets it, makes conjectures and hypotheses about it, and draws inferences from it to gain new information (Wellman 1988). In a recent study by Gopnik and Graf (1988), however, 4-year-old children were successful in very similar tasks.

Even in the middle school years, children who realize that one event can be interpreted differently by different people are nevertheless convinced that only one of these interpretations can be correct (Clinchy and Mansfield 1985; Enright and Lapsley 1980; Enright *et al.* 1984; Kuhn, Pennington, and Leadbeater 1983). Chandler (1988) argues from this that children in the middle school years still have the view that truth is objective and unitary; if one is in the right place at the right time with the right previous information, one will passively receive the truth. It is not until adolescence, says Chandler, that individuals come to the realization that knowledge is constructed, not passively received, and that it is partial, relative to one's history, position, and interests. It is at about this time that the common-sense view is first questioned by individuals. For the first time, they begin to entertain the sceptical suspicion that the relativity of knowledge to individual circumstances might call into question the very idea of a world of objective facts that we can certainly and unequivocally be said to know.

Part three
The Pathology of Common Sense

5

Representation and scepticism

We have seen that a representational model of the mind is embedded in the common-sense view of the world at a very deep level. It is a model that underwrites our ability to make the kind of metarepresentational distinctions outlined in Chapters 2 and 3. According to this model, which develops in each of us around the age of 4, the mind is essentially a 'representational organ': just as pretending that a banana is a telephone involves representing it as a telephone, just as imagining oneself riding a winged horse is a matter of representing oneself in a certain situation, so actually perceiving some object or situation in the world also involves representing it in a certain way. Furthermore, just as falsely believing that the drawer contains chocolate is to represent the world as being other than it is in fact, so in truly believing that the box contains pencils one comes to represent the world as it is. Our cognitive contact with the world, then, is mediated by the activity of mental representation, according to the common-sense model of the mind. But so is our behaviour, for our actions are not always a function of the way the world actually is; but it is, we believe, always a function of the way we think the world is, the way we represent it as being. Although the common-sense model of the mind is a representational model, the metaphysics embedded in common sense is, as we have seen in Chapter 1, uncompromisingly realist. It is a conception of the world as consisting of objects, events, and states of affairs that are independent of anyone's representation of them.

The marriage of a representational model of the mind's functioning and a realist metaphysics has proved to be a difficult one to sustain for some individuals. Chandler (1988) has reported that it is not at all untypical for adolescents and young adults, in reflecting on the relation between the mind and reality, to be led to sceptical doubts about our cognitive capacities, and about the very existence of a mind-independent reality and of objective truth. The source of whatever knowledge one has about the world, we think, is sense experience. Either we experience the objects and events themselves and observe their features and the relations in which they stand to other objects and events; or we acquire such knowledge via the testimony of others (i.e., by listening to them or by reading what they have written); or we gain new knowledge by inference from what we experience, together with knowledge we already have. But sense experience of the world is mediated by mental representation, according to the representational model of the mind. If one reflects on one's belief that all of one's cognitive contact with an external reality is mediated by mental representation, then it is likely to occur to one to ask potentially shattering questions: how can one ever be sure that one is representing reality accurately? In fact, one might come to think that one's only guarantee that there are other people, other representational beings, is the fact that one represents them oneself. But what kind of a guarantee is this? Indeed, how can one be sure that anything at all exists apart from one's own representational activity?

Such sceptical doubts may be manifestations of a pathological condition, a kind of intellectual illness that can be brought on by reflecting in a certain way on the common-sense view. On the other hand, the sceptical doubts may be symptoms of an emerging intellectual maturity, when genuine confusions, inadequacies, and contradictions inherent in the common-sense view are recognized for the first time. The naturally occurring philosophical disquiet of adolescence in fact closely resembles the kind of sustained theoretical critique of common sense that has been the hallmark of modern philosophical thought. This modern critique owes its origin and its guiding intellectual influence to Descartes, and it has developed within the framework of a theoretical model of the mind, also bequeathed to modern philosophy by Descartes, which is closely related to the representational model I have argued is bound up with common sense. Theoretical scepticism naturally arises within the context of Cartesian representationalism. In fact, I agree with Thomas Reid, the famous eighteenth-century defender of the common-sense view, that theoretical scepticism is the inescapable logical consequence of Cartesian representationalism.

It is my conviction that the sceptical doubts typical of adolescence are a pathological condition of the common-sense view, brought about by thinking of the phenomenon of mental representation essentially in the same way that Descartes did. But, I shall argue, common-sense representationalism is not committed to the Cartesian model of mental representation. Like Descartes himself and the modern philosophers who have subscribed to his model of the mind, the adolescent who reflects on the relation between the mind and the external world is misled by the phenomenology of metarepresentation. To put it in philosophical jargon, Cartesian philosophers and adolescent sceptics jump to the conclusion that the phenomenology of consciousness is a guide to the ontology of the mind.

In this chapter it will be my task to outline the Cartesian model of the mind as it was developed by Descartes himself, and as some of its important consequences were explored by the classical empiricists, Locke, Berkeley, and Hume, all of whom subscribed to the essential features of the Cartesian model, despite their disagreements with him, and with one another, on other important questions. The following chapter will concentrate on Thomas Reid's critique of the Cartesian model, and his defence of the common-sense view of the world against the sceptical consequences that he argued were inevitable consequences of adopting the Cartesian model. Reid recognized the untoward consequences of Cartesian representationalism, but he too failed to mount a convincing defence of common sense. Chapter 7 will investigate the curious case of G.E. Moore, who defended common sense while simultaneously remaining faithful to the Cartesian model. His defence of common sense, I shall argue, ultimately collapses precisely because he could not free himself from the essentially Cartesian view that the phenomenology of consciousness recapitulates the ontology of the mind's relation to the world. My overall aim in these chapters is to pave the way for my own defence of the common-sense view by showing that the common-sense view is not committed to the version of representationalism that has haunted western philosophy with the spectre of scepticism ever since Descartes

The Cartesian model of the mind

Descartes

The Cartesian model of the mind relies heavily on the metarepresentational ability to attend to the phenomenological features of consciousness: i.e., those features we are able to identify and describe merely by inspection of our present conscious state. It does so as a result of the methodological requirements of Descartes's search for the foundations of knowledge. Genuine knowledge, he thought, is distinguished from more-or-less probable opinion by the absolute certainty of the former. Unless there is a guarantee of its truth, a belief does not count as knowledge. Now anything which can, without self-contradiction or absurdity, be doubted, might possibly be false, no matter how strongly we are inclined to believe it. So Descartes resolved

> to accept nothing as true which I did not clearly recognize to be so: that is to say, carefully to avoid precipitation and prejudice in judgments, and to accept in them nothing more than was presented to my mind so clearly and distinctly that I could have no occasion to doubt it.
>
> (*Discourse on Method*, Part II)[1]

The beliefs I acquire as a result of sense experience have no guarantee of truth. In fact, I sometimes mistake the way things appear for the way they really are, as when I judge that the round tower which looks square to me from here really is square. I could, of course, take care not to make precipitate judgements, but Descartes argues that no amount of care will be sufficient to remove all source of doubt from sense experience; for when I am dreaming, the character of my dream experience is frequently indistinguishable from normal waking experience. If it were not, no one would ever be bothered by nightmares. But this is a source of general, wholesale doubt: there is nothing about my sense experiences *per se*, that is, the experiences which I believe are caused by objects in the world somehow acting on my sense organs, that marks them as genuine waking sense experiences. Thus, for any experience whatever, it is always possible for me to suppose without contradiction or absurdity that it is a dream experience and not a waking sense experience.

Even the most fundamental and obvious mathematical propositions are subject to systematic doubt. I am utterly convinced, subjectively certain, that the sum of the angles of any triangle are equal to two right angles, and that two and three together add up to five. But upon reflection I must admit, says Descartes, that an infinitely powerful but malicious being could deceive me in these matters, by so controlling my reasoning and judgmental capabilities as to convince me of the truth of these propositions even if they were not true. Even an infinitely powerful malicious being could not deceive me about my own existence, though. As long as I think I exist, I do exist. I could not possibly believe falsely that I exist. In fact, I must acknowledge that whenever I think in any way at all, I have therein a guarantee of my existence.

I know that I exist. The fact of my own existence is indubitable. But at this stage of the investigation, the only thing I can know about myself, about my own nature, is that I am a thinking thing, because my thoughts, whatever they are and however deceptive they might be, are simply and indubitably present to me. I am immediately conscious of my thoughts. No argument is needed to convince me that I have whatever thoughts I have at the time I have them; and no argument could possibly convince me that I do not have whatever thoughts are immediately present to my consciousness when I am conscious of them. But what does Descartes include within the realm of thoughts in saying that he is indubitably certain of any of his thoughts in so far as they are immediately present to consciousness?

> By the word *thought* I understand all that of which we are
> conscious as operating in us. And this is why not only
> understanding, willing and imagining but also feeling are here
> the same thing as thought.
>
> > (*Principles of Philosophy*, I, 10)

As Descartes uses these words, 'imagining' is any mental act in which an image is present to consciousness, 'understanding' is a mental act involving concepts, but not images. The difference may be illustrated by an example from the sixth of his *Meditations*. I can have the image of a many-sided regular polygon present to consciousness, for example when I think I am actually looking at one, or when I am merely 'conjuring up' one (what we ordinarily call 'imagination'). I cannot imagine the difference between a 999-sided regular polygon and a 1000-sided regular polygon. The images are indistinguishable. However, I can understand what a 999-sided regular polygon is, and I understand it to be different from a 1000-sided regular polygon. 'Feeling', as a form of thought, refers to the mental experience, immediately present to consciousness, of seeming to see, hear, taste, smell, or touch something. When I am dreaming that I am sitting near a fire, 'it is at least quite certain that it seems to me that I see light, that I hear noise, and that I feel heat' (*Meditations*, II); and in that sense I am immediately conscious of heat and light. 'This cannot be false; this is, properly speaking, what is in me called feeling; and used precisely in this sense it is no other thing than thinking' (*Meditations*, II). These experiences, these thoughts, are qualitatively indistinguishable from those I would have were I actually awake and sitting by the fire. That's why sense experiences, which in Descartes's terms are feelings (i.e., thoughts), are dubitable. It is possible to doubt whether the heat and light that I now feel, that I am now immediately conscious of, are actually caused by a situation in which I am actually sitting in front of a fire. But it is not possible to doubt that I am undergoing these experiences, while I am actually undergoing them, and in that sense I am thinking thoughts which are indubitable.

In *Meditations* III, Descartes surveys his thoughts and finds an internal distinction within each thought between the type of mental act involved (for example, affirming, denying, willing, fearing, imagining) and an object which is represented in the act. Descartes gives the technical name 'idea' to any such mentally represented object, saying that ideas are 'as it were images of things'. The analogy with images is very problematic, however. It is tempting to describe ourselves as having images of things (or as-it-were-images) present to consciousness when we are engaged in, or undergoing, one of the mental acts Descartes classifies as imagining or feeling. But his division of thoughts into an act component and an idea component is quite general, applying not only to imagination and feeling, but to purely conceptual thought as well; and it is difficult, to say the least, to conceive of some Cartesian ideas, for example the idea we have of God, on the analogy with images. In fact, Descartes specifically denies that our idea of God is an image. It is, though, an object before the mind.

Nevertheless, this much at least of Descartes's intention is clear: (a) ideas are *mental* objects, objects immediately present to consciousness in any mental act; (b) ideas are *representational* objects; it is their nature to stand for – or perhaps better, stand *in* for – extramental objects and situations. Whether I am actually looking at a fire or only dreaming that I am looking at one, I nevertheless have an idea present to my mind which is a representation of a fire. It is important to point out quite forcefully that the 'of' in the expression 'representation of a fire' does not imply that a relation holds between the idea (the representational object) and some actual fire. If I am actually looking at a fire, then there is some such relation brought about by the causal process of perception. But if I am only dreaming of a fire, then *ex hypothesi* there is no actual fire, and hence no relation between the idea and some actual fire. Thus, it is perhaps prudent to employ the terminology used by Nelson Goodman in his (1968) general investigation of representation, and say that what Descartes calls my idea of a fire is a fire-representation, which may or may not represent some actual fire, just as the famous series of tapestries in the Musée de Cluny in Paris are unicorn-representations, though there are no unicorns for them to be related to.

Descartes's analysis of thoughts into mental acts (acts of thinking) and mental objects (ideas) relies entirely on introspective, or phenomenological, evidence. If one carefully attends to one's present state of consciousness, one will simply be presented with one's current mental acts and their corresponding ideas. These are the phenomenologically obvious ingredients of consciousness, just obviously and self-evidently *there*. No argument or evidence is required in order to convince us of their presence; they are in this sense autonomous features of our conscious life. What is not at all obvious, for Descartes, in fact what is very problematic if the only things immediately present to consciousness are my own thoughts, is whether any extramental world exists apart from myself and my mental acts and ideas. Any knowledge I can possibly have of anything existing outside the circle of my own ideas must be mediated by, and grounded in, the ideas that are immediately present in consciousness.

Some of my ideas I am inclined to believe are accurate or true representations of external objects. That is to say, I am inclined to judge that they have extramental causes which resemble them, as when I take myself to be looking at a fire and not merely dreaming of one or imagining one. My ideas in these cases, I am inclined to believe, are internal, mental replicas of external physical objects. But in these cases I might actually be dreaming, or I might be the dupe of a malevolent deceiver. No matter how improbable the hypothesis that I am dreaming or universally deceived may seem to me, I cannot know that any of my ideas truly represent features of a world external to my consciousness unless I have a guarantee that those very ideas are true representations.

Descartes's own solution to the spectre of scepticism, which involved proving the existence of God and proving that it is inconsistent with God's benevolence to give us wholly deceptive inclinations to believe that our ideas truly represent external things, need not detain us. Suffice it to say that virtually all of his contemporaries and successors have thought it a failure. What is of crucial importance is the fact that Descartes's model of the mind, his 'theory of ideas', according to which the only objects of which we are immediately conscious are mental objects (ideas), which stand for objects outside the mind, has dominated modern thought.

Locke

John Locke, generally regarded as the founder of British empiricism, quarrelled with Descartes principally over the question of the origin of our ideas, but his strong adherence to the basic features of the Cartesian model of the mind was a central element in his philosophy. In the Introduction to his major work, the *Essay Concerning Human Understanding*, he defines an idea as 'whatever it is which the mind can be employed about in thinking'. Thus all thought, for Locke, has ideas as its only objects. Any knowledge we have about a world outside the circle of our ideas must be mediated by, and justified in terms of, knowledge we can have of our ideas themselves and their interrelations.

Locke did contribute some refinements to the theory of ideas, and some of the most problematic aspects of this model of the mind are highlighted by his struggles to give a satisfactory account of human knowledge in terms of its constraints. Whereas Descartes had argued that some of our ideas are innate, most particularly the idea of God, which is the ultimate ground of human knowledge in Cartesian rationalism, Locke argued that the source of all our ideas is experience: either sense experience, which provides us with 'ideas of sensation', or our experience of the operations of our own mind, which is the source of our 'ideas of reflection'.

Locke further distinguishes, within each of these classes of ideas, between those ideas which are simple, being both unanalysable and received in the mind passively, and complex ideas, which are actively formed by the mind by combining together simple ideas. Simple ideas of sensation include the ideas of the fragrant scent and the red colour of a petunia. Locke gives as examples of simple ideas of reflection the ideas of perception and of willing. By combining the simple ideas of fragrant scent, red colour, and other simple ideas of sensation, the mind actively forms the complex idea of a petunia. Similarly, complex ideas of reflection, such as the idea of beauty, are formed by the mind by combining simple ideas of reflection.

Our ideas of sensation are so called because their source, says Locke, is the action of things in the physical world on our sense organs. Corresponding to our ideas of sensation, therefore, are various qualities in the things around us.

> Whatsoever the mind perceives in itself or is the immediate object of perception, thought or understanding, that I call idea; and the power to produce any idea in our mind I call quality of the subject wherein that power is.

> (*Essay*, II,8,8)[2]

Our ideas of sensation, then, represent these qualities of physical objects. In sense perception, the qualities of the objects produce in us ideas. Our only objects of awareness are the ideas, from which we infer, albeit unconsciously, the existence of the objects and the resemblance of the qualities to our ideas of them. This basic outline of a representational account of perception Locke shared with Descartes. In addition, both of them made a distinction between two sorts of qualities in order to account for what they took to be a naïve error in the common person's conception of the nature of the perceived world.

Some qualities are invariant components of a physical object, no matter what changes it undergoes. 'These I call original or primary qualities of body, which I think we may observe to produce simple ideas in us, viz. solidity, extension, figure, motion or rest, and number' (*Essay*, II,8,9). Our ideas of primary qualities really do resemble the qualities themselves, and so what Locke takes to be our common-sense inferences that external objects resemble our ideas of them are correct in the case of our ideas of primary qualities. Our ideas of colours, tastes, sounds, odours, warmth, and cold, however, are quite different. If I place my left hand in a pail of cold water, my right hand in a pail of hot water, and then place both hands in a third pail of water, one hand will feel hot and the other cold; yet the water cannot be both hot and cold simultaneously. Similarly, the claret that tasted so marvellously full and rich just a moment ago will taste thin and bitter after I have had a bite of salad with vinaigrette dressing; yet it is the same claret. For reasons such as these, Locke thinks that we must conclude that our ideas of these so-called secondary qualities do not resemble anything actually existing in the objects which produce the ideas in us. What we call colours, tastes, and so on

> are, in the bodies we denominate from them, only a power to produce those sensations in us; and what is sweet, blue or warm in idea is but the certain bulk, figure and motion of the insensible parts in the bodies themselves, which we call so.
>
> (*Essay*, II,8,15)

Our common-sense belief that objects really are coloured, really do emit sounds and fragrances, and so on, is therefore mistaken, in so far as it is the belief that objects in the world resemble our ideas of them in these respects. In another sense, of course, objects really are coloured, and so on; for they really do have the power, in virtue of the arrangement of their 'insensible parts', to produce these ideas in us. Locke, along with Descartes, takes our common-sense beliefs to be beliefs about the relations of resemblance between our ideas and external objects.

Within the framework of the theory of ideas Locke took over from Descartes, according to which the only things immediately present to the mind are ideas, this way of construing common-sense beliefs is inevitable. For this model of the mind requires that all beliefs have ideas as their objects. But if our ideas are our only objects, how can Locke explain our ever having ideas of extramental qualities of objects, or indeed of extramental objects? It seems that Locke, in providing an explanation of the source of our ideas, and of the relation between our ideas and the extramental world, helps himself to an explanatory standpoint that is not available to any being who is limited to an acquaintance with his own ideas. Locke states confidently that some of our ideas resemble qualities in bodies and others do not; but how could he possibly be in a position to know how ideas are related to things which are not ideas? Berkeley, as we shall see, makes precisely this epistemological point in criticism of Locke, and draws a surprising metaphysical conclusion from it.

The sceptical seeds inherent in the Cartesian model of the mind become painfully evident in Locke's attempt to account for our ideas of physical things themselves, and not merely of their various qualities. In reflecting on the simple ideas we have of a certain shade of red, a certain fragrance, a certain shape, and the fact that they occur together as a kind of collectivity, we form the complex idea of a particular physical object, this petunia. Our idea of a particular thing, then, is the complex of a particular collection of simple qualities, the simple ideas of which we associate together. 'It is by such combinations of simple ideas, and nothing else, that we represent particular sorts of substances to ourselves' (*Essay*, II,23,6). However, in addition to the ideas we have of particular substances, we have also a general idea of substance. It is not merely the idea of this, that, or the other particular thing, but the idea of what a physical thing is *per se*, for in reflecting on our simple ideas of sensation which we associate together, we are struck by the fact that ideas of qualities, both primary and secondary, are never found in isolation, but always in such bundles as we think of as material things. Thus, 'not imagining how these simple ideas can subsist by themselves, we accustom ourselves to suppose some substratum wherein they do subsist and from which they do result; which therefore we call substance' (*Essay*, II,23,1). But how can we account for this general idea of substance? Our complex ideas of particular substances are nothing more than associated collections of simple ideas formed by reflection. There is nothing in such complex ideas that cannot be found in the simple ideas which compose them. The general idea of substance, however, the idea of 'the supposed but unknown support of those qualities we find existing' (*Essay*, 2,23,2), contains something not to be found in any of the simple ideas which form our complex ideas of particular substances. Locke says that it is formed by abstraction. But abstraction, in his view, is the activity of separating out a common feature from a number of ideas, and this cannot be the explanation of how we come to have the general idea of substance. Yet the idea of substance is supposed to be our *Representation and scepticism* idea of independently existing extramental things. It could not, therefore, be acquired via abstraction. Since Locke denies that we have any innate ideas, the origin in experience of the idea of something of which we can have no experience cannot be explained. Indeed, the very intelligibility of such an idea is problematic within the framework of the Cartesian model of the mind.

The Cartesian model is also responsible for the great difficulties Locke has in explaining how we can ever be justified in claiming to know anything about a world external to thought. His difficulties in this regard are compounded by the fact that he does not have recourse, as Descartes did, to the benevolence of God to guarantee that any of his ideas truly represent external things. 'Seeing the mind in all its thoughts and reasonings hath no other immediate object but its own ideas, which alone it does or can contemplate, it is evident that our knowledge is only conversant about them' (*Essay*, IV,1,1). So begins Book Four of the *Essay*. But Locke himself soon recognizes the problem inherent in this version of representationalism.

> It is evident that the mind knows not things immediately, but only by the intervention of the ideas it has of them. Our knowledge therefore is real only so far as there is a conformity between our ideas and the reality of things. But what shall be here the criterion? How shall the mind, when it perceives nothing but its own ideas, know that they agree with things themselves?
>
> (*Essay*, IV,4,3)

Locke's answer, in brief, is that our simple ideas of sensation are imposed on our minds; we do not actively create them ourselves. They must, therefore, be the result of something external to the mind acting upon us, and the ideas must therefore be in conformity to those things. Complex ideas, being formed of simple ideas, pose no insuperable additional problem, if the simple ideas conform to what produces them. The answer is question-begging, and need not detain us further. The important point is that no satisfactory answer is possible to Locke's question, given the Cartesian model of the mind to which he subscribes. If there are objects external to and independent of the mind, our ideas might well conform to them, although it is difficult to conceive of what 'conformity' might amount to, since resemblance has been ruled out, in the case of ideas of secondary qualities at any rate. But we could never be in a position to know whether our ideas in fact conformed to these

95

objects or not. In fact, as Berkeley so forcefully argued, if the mind perceives nothing but its own ideas, we could never be in a position even to entertain the possibility that there is anything for our ideas to conform to.

Berkeley

In one respect, Berkeley's philosophy is a radical departure from Descartes and Locke, in that he recognized, and traced in detail, the unpalatable implications of their doctrine that ideas are mental entities the function of which is to represent extramental reality. In rejecting their representationalism, however, he by no means rejected the underlying theory of ideas, the view that the only objects of which the mind is immediately conscious are ideas. His departure from Descartes and Locke was in actually identifying the ordinary objects we perceive and think about as ideas. Since ordinary objects are ideas, we perceive them directly. No mediation is either required or possible. In this claim, Berkeley takes himself to be echoing the view of 'plain common sense'. What are Berkeley's reasons for such an extraordinary doctrine?

One important argument is his refutation of the Lockean notion of physical things as mind-independent substances which support a variety of sensible qualities. First, he demolishes Locke's argument for the distinction between ideas and qualities of objects. Locke's reason for denying that there is anything in bodies actually resembling our ideas of colour, sound, taste, smell, warmth, and cold was that our sensations, for example the warmth we feel, the red we see, the loud noise we hear, are relative to the conditions under which we acquire these sensations, but we cannot suppose there to be qualities independently existing in the external objects that vary as our sensations vary. The water in the pail cannot actually be both hot and cold at the same time, though it is felt to be so. But, Berkeley argues, exactly the same is true of the socalled primary qualities. The shape a penny appears to be, our visual idea of it, changes as we move about in relation to the coin; but we cannot suppose that the penny is continually changing shape, as we would have to if our ideas of primary qualities resembled qualities actually inhering in the objects. Berkeley concludes from this that ideas don't represent qualities; they *are* those qualities. And since it is admitted that ideas are subjective, mental entities, it follows that all qualities of objects are ideas before the mind. The warmth we feel really exists, as does the red we see. The error lies in thinking that these are just representations of something that exists unperceived. Locke was right when he said that our complex ideas of particular things are collections of simple ideas which we associate together. His mistake was in thinking that we have, in addition, the idea of something completely unperceived and unperceivable which holds together and supports the ideas of the particular qualities. Mind-independent material substance is, in fact, inconceivable, since our only objects are ideas. So-called material things are nothing other than collections of ideas.

Although Berkeley thought he was defending plain common sense with his idealist philosophy, he was aware that ordinary people do not believe that the familiar objects they perceive are collections of ideas whose existence is dependent upon their being perceived. 'It is indeed an opinion strangely prevailing amongst men, that houses, mountains, rivers, and in a word all sensible objects have an existence natural or real, distinct from their being perceived by the understanding' (*Principles*, 1,4).[3] Berkeley is of course right. Our concept of a material object is the concept of something the existence of which is in no way dependent on anyone's perceiving it. Nevertheless, since our ideas are the only objects of which we are conscious, the strangely prevailing opinion is contradictory.

> For what are the aforementioned objects but the things we perceive by sense, and what do we perceive besides our own ideas or sensations; and is it not plainly repugnant that any one of these or any combination of them should exist unperceived?
>
> (*Principles*, 1,4)

If we will but reflect on what we really mean by the word 'exists' when we apply it to so-called material objects, which Berkeley preferred to call 'sensible objects', we will be less inclined to insist that these objects exist unperceived.

> The table I write on, I say, exists, that is, I see and feel it; and if I were out of my study I should say it existed, meaning thereby that if I was in my study I might perceive it, or that some other spirit actually does perceive it.
>
> (*Principles*, 1,3)

In claiming that this captures all that we really mean when we say that things exist, Berkeley subscribes to the phenomenalist analysis that was taken up again by John Stuart Mill (1872) in the nineteenth century and was developed extensively by philosophers such as Russell (1917), Price (1940), Ayer (1940), and Lewis (1947), during the early years of the present century. But does the phenomenalist formulation really capture all we mean when we say that the table exists? It is arguable that it captures all the *empirical consequences* of the claim that the table exists. But that is not the same thing as capturing what we mean, what sort of claim we are making, when we make the common-sense claim that the table exists, independently of my or anyone else's perception or thought. As to Berkeley's argument that the common-sense belief is contradictory, it rests entirely on the Cartesian model of the mind according to which we are aware only of our own ideas; or as Berkeley formulated it in the passage quoted above, it rests on the view that we perceive nothing except our own ideas and sensations.

Hume

Descartes provided the theoretical framework; Locke put his finger on the problem; Berkeley diagnosed representational ideas as the culprit, but by remaining faithful to ideas as objects before the mind he failed to pursue the sceptical consequences of the Cartesian model of the mind, constructing instead his own extraordinary metaphysics of ideas. It remained to Hume to demonstrate the full sceptical implications of the theory of ideas, but he too didn't see the necessity of re-examining the model of the mind that provides the seeds of its own sceptical demise.

Like Locke and Berkeley before him, Hume insists that all of the mind's contents have their source in experience. The general term he uses to designate anything before the mind is 'perception', and he divides all the perceptions of the mind into impressions and ideas. The former correspond to Locke's 'simple ideas': they are the primary ingredients of experience. The latter are copies or images of the former.

> The difference betwixt these consists in the degrees of force and liveliness with which they strike upon the mind and make their way into our thoughts or consciousness. Those perceptions which enter with most force and violence we may name *impressions*; and under this name, I comprehend all our sensations, passions and emotions. By *ideas* I mean the faint images of these in thinking and reasoning.
>
> (*Treatise*, I,1,1)[4]

Again following a basically Lockean line, Hume divides impressions into two kinds: impressions of sensation and those of reflection. Although Hume's language in the passage quoted above, the imagery of striking and entering, suggests that impressions have an origin external to the mind, Hume is very careful not to beg such an important question. 'The first kind arises in the soul originally from unknown causes (*Treatise*, I,1,2). Impressions of sensation can leave a copy in the mind, an idea, which may later be remembered, and which may be combined with other ideas to form complex ideas to which no impressions ever corresponded, as when one imagines a centaur, by combining ideas derived from one's impressions of men and of horses. But impressions of sensation can also give rise to impressions of reflection, as when an impression of pain leaves behind a copy (the idea or thought of pain), which in turn gives rise to an impression of aversion.

Hume's taxonomy of 'perceptions' is of great significance in his version of empiricism. Since impressions are the ultimate source of all ideas, any idea one professes to have must be traceable to some antecedent impression or impressions. Similarly, any empirical (i.e., fact-asserting) proposition one believes (as opposed to logical or mathematical propositions having to do merely with the relations among ideas) must be justified by reference to impressions.

Take, for example, our belief in the existence of bodies external to and independent of our minds (i.e., independent of and external to our impressions and ideas). He agrees with Berkeley's criticism of Lockean material substance: the idea we allegedly have of substance cannot be derived from any impression of sensation; for the whole role of the so-called idea of substance is to denote the supposed unperceived support of perceived qualities. But neither is it derivable from any impression of reflection, according to Hume. Therefore, we have no such idea. The alleged idea of substance is 'nothing but a collection of simple ideas that are united by the imagination and have a particular name assigned to them, by which we are able to recall, either to ourselves or others, that collection' (*Treatise*, I,1,6). But neither can we justify the belief that these collections of ideas correspond to, or are caused by, any external, continuously existing, mind-independent entities, such as we suppose ordinary objects to be. The existence of continuously existing mind-independent entities cannot be demonstrated logically, since the denial of any proposition asserting the existence of an external body is by no means self-contradictory. But neither can we have a sense impression which guarantees the independent, continuous, external existence of any body. A body exists continuously if it exists even when it is not being perceived. It is not self-contradictory to suppose that the objects of (i.e., present to us in) our impressions cease to exist when we cease to have the impressions; and of course we can have no impression of something's existing when we are not having an impression of it.

In fact, a sober reflection on the nature of the mind and its capabilities reveals that there can be no justification whatever for our belief in, or even the intelligible conception of, the existence of bodies independent of perception.

> Now since nothing is ever present to the mind but perceptions, and since all ideas are derived from something antecedently present to the mind, it follows that it is impossible for us so much as to conceive or form an idea of anything specifically different from ideas and impressions. Let us fix our attention on ourselves as much as possible; let us chase our imagination to the heavens, or to the utmost limits of the universe; we never really advance a step beyond ourselves, nor can conceive any kind of existence, but those perceptions which have appeared in that narrow compass.
>
> (*Treatise*, I,2,6)

We cannot provide a rational justification for our belief in the existence of external things, then, according to Hume. Nevertheless such a belief is universal, and Hume thinks he can provide a psychological explanation of why we come to have such an unfounded belief. Briefly stated, his view is that this belief is the product of our imagination. The constant and coherent occurrence of impressions in certain patterns produce in us collections of ideas that we associate together and through habit come to expect to continue occurring together.

> Those mountains and houses and trees which lie at present under my eye have always appeared to me in the same order; and when I lose sight of them by shutting my eyes or turning my head, I soon after find them returning to me without the least alteration.
>
> (*Treatise*, I,4,2)

This is what he means by the constant occurrence of certain groups of impressions together. The following is an example of what Hume means by saying that our impressions form coherently altering patterns.

> When I return to my chamber after an hour's absence, I find not my fire in the same situation in which I left it; but then I am accustomed, in other instances, to see a like alteration produced in a like time, whether I am present or absent, near or remote.
>
> (*Treatise*, I,4,2)

But from these patterns in our experience, no inference is justified to the effect that some continuously existing body produces them. The belief in continuously existing external bodies is entirely a product of our imagination. 'The imagination, when it is set into any train of thinking, is apt to continue even when its object fails it, and, like a galley put in motion by the oars, carries on its course without any new impulse' (*Treatise*, I,4,2). This habitual association, though it does not justify the inference of an independently existing external reality, in fact leads us to imagine (to 'feign') such a continuous existence. Thus, nature provides for us where reason is impotent. We cannot help believing in the existence of mind-independent, continuously existing bodies, but the belief is not justified on either logical or empirical grounds.

In this chapter I have attempted to outline the commitment to a particular conception of the mind on the part of some of the most important philosopher-psychologists of the seventeenth and eighteenth centuries, and how that commitment influenced their views about the relation between the mind and the objects we perceive and think about. In the case of each of these thinkers, the conception of the mind as immediately cognizant of mental entities with characteristics we commonly attribute to objects in the physical world, led them to pose the question of what the relationship can be between these mental entities and the familiar objects in the extramental world with which we commonly believe we are in perceptual contact. In answer to this question, Descartes and Locke took the view that the mental objects are representations, but not exact replicas, of external objects; Berkeley argued that the mental objects are the familiar objects of perception and thought; Hume's answer was that there can be no answer, given the sort of mind we humans have.

It did not occur to any of them to question the model of the mind that led to consequences so much at odds with common sense. Each of them was convinced that the basic nature of the mind is transparently evident to anyone who attends carefully to conscious experience. If conscious experience proves to be at odds with our common beliefs, so much the worse for our common beliefs. Berkeley genuinely thought that he was defending the common-sense view, of course; and in one respect he was, in his insistence that we perceive objects in the world themselves, not representations of them. But his view that these objects cannot exist unperceived is diametrically opposed to the common-sense view of objects as mind-independent entities.

It may well be that something like the Cartesian model is likely to seem transparently obvious to anyone who seriously and systematically reflects on his conscious experience. That may explain not only why it has seemed so compelling to Descartes and so many other philosophers of mind but also why young people during adolescence, when they begin to reflect about the nature of mind, tend to raise sceptical doubts about the common-sense view of the world that has guided their lives and will continue to do so in practice despite the doubts. But does it follow that the transparently obvious view is true? Thomas Reid thought not, and it is to his critique that we now turn.

6

Thomas Reid's defence of common sense

In Descartes's fall, sinned we all. This, at least, is what Locke, Berkeley, and Hume should have confessed, according to Thomas Reid, who diagnosed the sceptical implications of the Cartesian model of the mind in the course of presenting his own defence of common sense. It was this model of the mind, which he called 'the ideal philosophy', that Reid diagnosed as being chiefly responsible for philosophical scepticism, in large part owing to its ill-conceived neglect of the principles of common sense.

> The defects and blemishes in the received philosophy concerning the mind, which have most exposed it to the contempt and ridicule of sensible men, have chiefly been owing to this – that the votaries of this Philosophy, from a natural prejudice in her favour, have endeavoured to extend her jurisdiction beyond its just limits, and to call to her bar the dictates of Common Sense. But these decline this jurisdiction; they disdain the trial of reasoning, and disown its authority; they neither claim its aid nor dread its attacks.
>
> (*Inquiry*, I.iv)[1]

According to Descartes, our belief that there is a world external to and independent of our own ideas is supported by reason; it is a conclusion we can infer from our ideas with certainty, only because some elements of our ideas of objects are clear and distinct, and a benevolent God guarantees that all of our clear and distinct ideas are true. Locke, whose empiricism prevented him from grounding human knowledge of external objects in the benevolence of God, saw the spectre of scepticism looming, but argued (albeit very unconvincingly) that our reason does justify the belief that our ideas, at least our ideas of primary qualities, do truly represent external, mind-independent objects. Berkeley, recognizing that the hypothesis of mind-independent material substance is irrational, given the constraints of the theory of ideas, which he accepted without question, took the heroic course of

103

arguing that reason supports the doctrine that ordinary objects of perception are themselves collections of ideas. His sincere but erroneous insistence that this is what we all believe was met by the contemptuous stone-kicking refutation of Dr Johnson. It was left to Hume, a more astute philosopher than the eminent lexicographer, to demonstrate in painful detail that the theory of ideas, which he too unquestioningly accepted as the correct model of the mind, leads inexorably to scepticism with regard to our claims to know, or even to believe with rational justification, that there are objects external to and independent of our impressions and ideas. We can, Hume thought, provide a psychological explanation of how we come to have such beliefs; but we cannot justify them rationally.

But our common-sense beliefs, Reid was to argue, including our firm belief in the existence of a world of objects existing independently of our perception of them and our thoughts about them, are not grounded in reason, but in our nature. Hume was right to say that nature produces these beliefs in us; but the very fact that they arise in us naturally, for Reid, is ample justification for our insistence that they are a true and secure foundation for the knowledge claims we in turn justify by appealing to these common-sense beliefs. This is his principal disagreement with Hume. The beliefs of common sense constitute the secure principles *from* which we reason, not tenuous hypotheses *for* which we reason.

The nature of common sense

Common sense, according to Reid, is a network of beliefs, common in the sense that they are shared by all humankind (except very young infants, the feeble-minded, and the deranged), which underwrite our ability to communicate and reason with one another. 'Before men can reason together, they must agree in first principles, and it is impossible to reason with a man who has no principles in common with you' (*Essays*, I.ii). These beliefs appear in us very early in our lives. However, they are not acquired through instruction, but appear to be 'an immediate effect of our constitution' (*Essays*, VI.iv). It is in this sense that common-sense beliefs are *first principles* of reasoning.

> There are, therefore, common principles, which are the
> foundation of all reasoning and of all science. Such common
> principles seldom admit of direct proof, nor do they
> need it. Men need not to be taught them; for they are such as all

men of common understanding know; or such, at least, as they
give a ready assent to, as soon as they are proposed and
understood.

(Essays, I.ii)

And since we are under a kind of natural necessity of holding these
beliefs, Reid speaks of them as 'dictates'. 'For first principles no
other reason can be given but this, that, by the constitution of our
nature, we are under a necessity of assenting to them' (*Inquiry*,
V.vii).

> All reasoning is from principles. The first principles of mathe-
> matical reasoning are mathematical axioms and definitions;
> and the first principles of all our reasoning about existences are
> our perceptions. The first principles of every kind of reasoning
> are given us by nature, and are of equal authority with the
> faculty of reason itself, which is also a gift of nature.
>
> *(Inquiry*, VI.xx)

> Opinions that appear so early in the minds of men that they
> cannot be the effect of education or of false reasoning, have
> good claim to be considered as first principles. Thus the belief
> that we have, that the persons about us are living and intelligent
> beings, is a belief for which, perhaps, we can give some reason,
> when we are able to reason; but we had this belief before we
> could reason, and before we could learn by instruction. It
> seems, therefore, to be an immediate effect of our constitution.
>
> *(Essays*, VI.iv)

Not only are we under a natural necessity of holding the beliefs of
common sense, Reid thinks that they are so necessary in the
conduct of our everyday lives that without them we would not long
survive.

> When an opinion is so necessary to the conduct of life, that,
> without the belief of it, a man must be led into a thousand
> absurdities in practice, such an opinion, when we can give no
> other reason for it, may safely be taken for a first principle.
>
> *(Essays*, VI.iv)

> I gave implicit belief to the informations of Nature by my
> senses, for a considerable part of my life, before I had learned
> so much logic as to be able to start a doubt concerning them.
> And now, when I reflect upon what is past, I do not find that I
> have been imposed upon by this belief. I find that without it I
> must have perished by a thousand accidents.
>
> *(Inquiry*, VI.xx)

According to Reid, common sense is *common* in the sense of being widely, indeed virtually universally, shared. Since each of us shares these beliefs with others, and each of us also *believes* them to be shared with others, they form a set of expectations we bring to any interchange with others which underwrites our ability to communicate with them as fellow rational beings. If we could not anticipate that others shared a vast network of judgements with us, there would be no common ground to support our attempts to reason with one another or even to communicate.

> In common language, sense always implies judgment. A man of sense is a man of judgment. Good sense is good judgment. Nonsense is what is evidently contrary to right judgment. Common sense is that degree of judgment which is common to men with whom we can converse and transact business.
>
> (*Essays*, VI.ii)

To summarize the general characteristics of common sense according to Reid: the principles of common sense are a set of beliefs, usually implicit, common to virtually all humankind past the stage of infancy. Since they appeared in us before we could consider reasons for or against them, they cannot be the effect of false reasoning, or even of correct reasoning. They must, therefore, be principles we are innately determined to believe: they are not optional in our lives; we are under a necessity of assenting to them, even though we can give no reason (i.e., no independent logical justification) for holding them true. When we articulate them to ourselves, when we attend to them, they appear to us self-evident. Whatever is contrary to one of these beliefs is not considered merely false but absurd, since our ability to communicate intelligibly and intelligently with one another depends on our mutually attributing them to each other.

Having set forth the general characteristics of the principles of common sense, what are the actual beliefs that Reid thinks constitute common sense? Although he does not pretend to be able to give an exhaustive inventory, in the *Essays* (VI.iv) he does list a number of 'first principles of contingent truths', these being beliefs expressed by propositions which are not established by reflection on the mere meanings of the terms comprising them. These beliefs have empirical content. It is logically possible that they be false, for their negations are not self-contradictory; yet we accept them as first principles in the sense Reid outlined for us above. So we may take them as common-sense beliefs which have, according to Reid, a foundational role to play in relation to the various other empirical beliefs we come to have. Although not all of Reid's propositions are direct statements of features of the two components of common sense discussed in Chapter 1 – rational psychology and common-sense realism – each of them is at least indirectly implicated in one or the other of those components. Furthermore, and more importantly, it will be readily apparent that each of them presupposes one or more of the cognitive abilities outlined in Chapter 2. Reid's list is as follows.

1. 'Everything of which I am conscious exists.' This seems to be a very surprising claim to make on behalf of common sense, if 'exists' is taken to mean 'exists independently of consciousness'. Surely Reid did not intend to claim that imaginary creatures such as centaurs and unicorns exist? As we shall see, Reid denies that centaurs and the like are objects in (or before) the mind; they are ingredients in the mental operation of imagining or otherwise conceiving, but they are not, according to Reid, things of which I am conscious. But if we rule out so-called objects of imagination and other ingredients of consciousness, the only remaining things are the things in the physical world of which we are conscious when we perceive them and think about them. So the first principle really amounts to this banal claim: the (mind-independent) entities of which I am sometimes conscious exist (mind-independently). The only quarrel a sceptic would have with this principle is its implication that we are occasionally conscious of mind-independent entities. But this, the sceptic would argue, is not something we can know on the basis of an introspective examination of the contents of consciousness.

2. 'The thoughts of which I am conscious are the thoughts of myself.' That is, they are *my* thoughts; they are the thoughts of the person I call *myself*. This principle is directed against Hume, who argued (*Treatise*, I,4,6) that since the only contents of the mind are impressions and ideas, and I have no impression of myself, my only idea of myself is the idea of a 'bundle of perceptions'.

3. 'Those things did happen that I distinctly remember.' Here Reid is referring to the conviction that something is remembered. The word 'memory' is also used as a 'success' verb, according to which 'X really happened' follows from 'I remember x'. Under this use, of course, Reid's principle would be trivially true. But is it a fundamental principle, something we find undeniable in practice, that our distinct convictions that we remember something are always correct? Reid is more confident on this score than I am.

4. 'Our own personal identity and continued existence [is assured]

as far as we remember anything distinctly.' When in the grip of hyperbolic doubt, Descartes entertained the hypothesis that he existed intermittently, that is, only when he was conscious and was therefore thinking. He searched for a rational justification for the conviction that he exists continuously. One might also doubt whether one exists at any time other than now, and seek a rational justification for the belief that one existed in the past. Reid's claim is that one's conviction that one is a single continuously existing person is a principle from which we reason. It is not a hypothesis for which we need to find rational support.

5. 'Those things do really exist which we distinctly perceive with our senses, and are what we perceive them to be.' This, of course, is a fundamental constituent of common-sense realism, and the chief target of the scepticism inherent in the theory of ideas. One of the prime objectives of Reid's defence of common sense is to secure this principle against the view, held by Descartes, Locke, and Hume, though not by Berkeley, that things we perceive with our senses are not what we perceive them to be.

6. 'We have some degree of power over our actions and the determination of our will.' Here is Reid's comment on this principle, which we may take as expressing a constituent feature of common-sense rational psychology:

> It is not more evident that mankind have a conviction of the existence of the material world, than that they have the conviction of some degree of power in themselves and in others; everyone over his own actions, and the determination of his will – a conviction so early, so general and so interwoven with the whole of human conduct, that it must be the natural effect of our constitution, and intended by the Author of our being to guide our actions.... It resembles the conviction of the existence of a material world in this respect also, that even those who reject it in speculation, find themselves under a necessity of being governed by it in their practice; and thus it will always happen when philosophy contradicts first principles.

7. 'The natural faculties by which we distinguish truth from error are not fallacious.'

8. 'There is life and intelligence in our fellow human beings with whom we converse.' This belief appears in us very early, and though the 'problem of other minds' may persuade us that we have no justifiable reason to believe that those we take to be intelligent beings are not mere automata, the belief is indispensable in our

lives, and also in the lives of sceptics who profess not to know whether or not they are surrounded by automata.

> As soon as children are capable of asking a question, or of answering a question ... they must be convinced that those with whom they have this intercourse are intelligent.... It cannot be said that the judgments we form concerning life and intelligence are free from error. But the errors of children on this matter lie on the safe side; they are prone to attribute intelligence to things inanimate. These errors are of small consequence, and are soon corrected by experience and ripe judgment.

9. 'Certain features of the countenance, sounds of the voice, and gestures ... indicate certain thoughts and dispositions of the mind.' This we may take to be Reid's identification of another constituent feature of common-sense rational psychology, which we rely on in attributing epistemic and desiderative states to others as part of our explanations and anticipations of their behaviour.

10. 'There is a certain regard due to testimony in matters of fact ... and opinion.'

11. 'There are many events depending upon the will of man in which there is a self-evident probability.' That is, a great deal of human action is predictable. This is another feature of common-sense psychology, related to our conviction that people have some power over their actions (Principle no. 6) and our conviction that their behaviour is generally reliable as an indication of their desiderative and epistemic states (Principle no. 9).

12. 'The future will resemble the past.' Here is another response to Hume's famous argument (*Treatise*, I,3,12) that this belief of ours, which is so central to inductive inference, cannot be rationally justified.

Reid's defence of common sense

Reid has four distinct lines of defence of the beliefs of common sense against the sceptic, who argues that there is no rational justification for belief in a mind-independent (i.e., an external) world.

First, any argument the conclusion of which contradicts common sense must rest on one or more false premises or an error in reasoning. Since the principles of common sense are an innately determined set of beliefs that guide our lives and are a pre-supposed background to all rational intercourse; since we reason *from* them and not *for* them; they are, claims Reid, immune to any criticism directed towards them from the point of view of some metaphysical or epistemological theory, or some model of the mind, which has been constructed according to the dictates of reason (i.e., has been constructed by people drawing the logical consequences of premises that seem theoretically convincing to them).

> The province of common sense is more extensive in refutation than in confirmation. A conclusion drawn by a train of just reasoning from true principles cannot possibly contradict any decision of common sense, because truth will always be consistent with itself. Neither can such a conclusion receive any confirmation from common sense, because it is not within its jurisdiction.
>
> But it is possible that, by setting out from false principles, or by an error in reasoning, a man may be led to a conclusion that contradicts the decisions of common sense. In this case, the conclusion is within the jurisdiction of common sense, though the reasoning on which it was grounded be not; and a man of common sense may fairly reject the conclusion without being able to shew the error of the reasoning that led to it.
>
> (*Essays*, VI.ii)

This argument is virtually identical to one used by G.E. Moore in defence of a certain class of common-sense beliefs. Since I will be examining Moore's argument in some detail in the next chapter, I shall not pause here to assess Reid's use of it.

Second, both common sense and the power of reason are gifts of nature. Therefore, there is no more reason to believe that the former is inherently defective than the latter.

> The sceptic asks me, Why do you believe the existence of the external object when you perceive? This belief, sir, is none of my manufacture; it came from the mint of Nature; it bears her image and superscription; and if it is not right, the fault is not mine.... Reason, says the sceptic, is the only judge of truth, and you ought to throw off every opinion and every belief that is not grounded on reason. Why, sir, should I believe the faculty of reason more than that of perception? – they came both out of the same shop, and were made by the same artist; and if he puts one piece of false ware into my hands, what should hinder him from putting another?
>
> (*Inquiry*, VI.xx)

This is not a very convincing argument. The sceptic only needs to point out, by way of reply, that the 'faculty of perception' is not without its defects. Not only are congenital infirmities such as poor eyesight and defective hearing products of 'the mint of Nature'; in ordinary life our inborn perceptual apparatus sometimes leads us to believe that external objects exist which either don't exist at all (hallucinations), or don't have the characteristics Nature seems to constrain us to believe them to have (illusions). The fact that the 'faculty of Reason' fares no better is rather cold comfort. Hume, in fact, argued that the faculty of Reason is incapable of guaranteeing the truth of our belief in material objects. But neither can 'the faculty of Perception' guarantee the truth of the beliefs it imposes upon us. If both faculties are 'pieces of false ware', then we are doubly disadvantaged.

Third, the sceptic is involved in an inconsistency if he admits that what is immediately present to consciousness (one's own ideas) is known, and can serve as a premiss for epistemological reasoning, but goes on to reject as knowledge the testimony of memory, or what is immediately present to the senses in perception.

> The greatest sceptics admit the testimony of consciousness, and
> allow that what it testifies is to be held as a first principle. If,
> therefore, they reject the immediate testimony of the senses or
> of memory, they are guilty of an inconsistency.
>
> (*Essays*, VI.iv)

This argument is bound up with Reid's critique of the theory of ideas, which he thinks is largely responsible for sceptical doubts concerning common sense. According to the theory of ideas, the only objects the existence of which consciousness testifies for are mental objects: our ideas. Reid's argument is that, contrary to the claim of the theorist of ideas, consciousness does testify to the existence of material objects, in that our nature constrains us to believe we are actually conscious of external, independently existing objects. The theorist of ideas is misled by his own model of the mind, which misconstrues the nature of consciousness. We will examine this argument when we turn to Reid's critique of the theory of ideas.

Fourth, the sceptic refutes himself by acting in everyday life on the very beliefs he repudiates when on official duty in his sceptic's uniform.

> The sceptic may perhaps persuade himself, in general, that he
> has not ground to believe his senses or his memory; but, in
> particular cases ... his disbelief vanishes, and he finds himself
> under a necessity of believing both.
>
> (*Essays,* VI.i)

> Even those who reject [the existence of a material world] in
> speculation, find themselves under a necessity of being gov-

erned by it in their practice; and thus it will always happen when philosophy contradicts first principles.

(*Essays*, VI.v)

This argument, in the form in which Reid advances it, amounts to nothing more than an *ad hominem*: the sceptic does not, and cannot, practise what he preaches, an observation which Hume freely admitted. But Hume would go on to argue, with justice, that our psychological compulsion to believe does not in itself amount to a justification of the claim that these beliefs are true.

Reid's critique of the theory of ideas

If the conclusion of a philosophical argument is absurd by the light of common sense, says Reid, then we have a right to reject that conclusion. As we saw in the previous chapter, the ideal theory, Reid's label for the Cartesian model of the mind, leads to the conclusion that we have no rational justification for believing in the existence of a mind-independent world of physical objects. This conclusion is absurd by the light of common sense. Therefore, we have a right to reject the ideal theory, even if it is impossible to determine just where that theory has erred. But in fact, Reid thinks he can point out where the theory of ideas has gone wrong. Its fatal defects lie in its conception of the nature of sensations (which according to the ideal theory are a species of ideas), and in the role it attributes to sensations in the fixation of our perceptual beliefs.

It is the reification of sensations, the construing of sensations as mental entities, that is the principal source of these sceptical consequences, according to Reid. The ideal theorists confuse an act or operation of the mind, which in Reid's view is the proper way to conceive of sensation, with an object before the mind. A sensation is a subjective experience, such as one has when one perceives some object. In perceiving via the having of sensations, the sensation is the *way* in which one experiences the object one perceives. But it is not an object in its own right which *is* experienced. 'In sensation, there is no object distinct from the act of the mind by which it is felt – and this holds true with regard to all sensations' (*Essays*, II.xvi).

This is, however, a confusion to which it is extraordinarily easy to fall prey, and this for several reasons. First, sensations are what were called in Chapter 2 first-order mental representations; they are the ways in which we represent the objects and situations in the world that we perceive. In normal perception, our focus of attention is on the objects and events we perceive via the sensations we have. It is unusual, and even difficult, for us to attend to, to metarepresent, our own sensations as we are having them. Sensations do their work as mental operations without our typically attending to them in any way, much less considering them as evidence from which to make inferences as to the existence and qualities of external objects.

> This sensation of hardness may be easily had, by pressing one's hand against the table, and attending to the feeling that ensues.... But it is one thing to have a sensation, and another to attend to it, and make it a distinct object of reflection. The first is very easy; the last, in most cases, very difficult.
>
> (*Inquiry*, V.ii)

> So difficult is it to attend properly even to our own feelings [i.e., our sensations]. They are accustomed to pass through the mind unobserved, and instantly make way for that which nature intended them to signify, that it is difficult to stop and survey them.
>
> (*Inquiry*, V.viii)

But to say that it is difficult to attend to our sensations (and also other 'operations of the mind') is only to say that we do not normally or easily *reflect* on them. The distinction Reid has in mind here is, I think, the same as that I have called the distinction between first-order and second-order mental representation in Chapter 2. 'It is in our power ... to give attention to our own thoughts and passions, and the various operations of our minds. And when we make these the object of our attention ... this act is called *reflection*' (*Essays*, I.ii).

> This reflection ought to be distinguished from consciousness.... All men are conscious of the operations of their own minds, at all times, while they are awake; but there are few who reflect upon them, or make them the objects of thought.
>
> (*Essays*, I.v)

Perhaps one reason that we do not normally reflect on our sensations and other operations of our minds is that very fact that they are operations, not objects; they are, so to speak, mental doings, not mental things. When we do reflect on one of these operations, it becomes 'a distinct object of reflection'. But an object of reflection is simply the topic, or focus, of reflection; it is not necessarily an object in the stronger sense of being a kind of entity one is inspecting. Thinking of sensations as objects in their own right, indeed as the only objects immediately and non-inferentially present to the mind when we take ourselves to be perceiving objects in the world, naturally produces the problem of accounting for the relation between these objects and those other objects in the world outside the mind. The ideal theorist evidently mistakes the metarepresentional operation of reflecting on one's act of representing an external object (the object of reflection) for a mental entity (object) thereby present to the mind. If this mental entity is not itself the only object in perception (Berkeley's gambit, followed by Hume), then it must be a kind of representational image of the external object (Descartes's and Locke's gambit). But if sensations aren't conceived of as objects before the mind, but rather as operations of the mind by which the mind represents the objects it perceives, our model of the mind does not prevent us from identifying the external objects themselves as the only objects with which the mind is in cognitive contact in perception. The mind is still thought of as a representational organ, but we have freed ourselves from image-thinking, from reification of sensations as mental objects. Reid shows how we can have a representational theory of the mind without representational objects. This basically *direct realist* account of perception is the one championed by Reid as the common-sense view. As we shall see, however, he is not entirely consistent in his devotion to direct realism.

Even when we manage to reflect on our sensations and other mental operations, our language encourages us to reify them. Here one source of confusion lies in the semantics, what Reid calls the 'dual signification', of the expressions we use to designate our sensations. Typically, the same word is used to refer both to the sensation (a momentary, subjective experiencing) and to the quality of an object, or feature of a situation, one perceives by means of the sensation. For example, when one feels cold things (that is, things that are cold) one usually feels cold (that is, one has a cold sensation; that is, one has a sensation of cold).

> The sensation I feel, and the quality in the rose which I perceive, are both called by the same name. The smell of a rose is the name given to both: so that this name hath two meanings; and the distinguishing its different meanings removes all perplexity.... All the names we have for smells, tastes, sounds, and for the various degrees of heat and cold, have a like ambiguity ... they signify both a sensation and a quality perceived by means of that sensation.
>
> (*Essays*, II.xvi)

In this respect Reid's view resembles that of Locke. But unlike Locke, Reid is not tempted to explicate the relation between sensations and the qualities of which they are sensations in terms of the notion of resemblance.

> The words *heat* and *cold* have each of them two significations; they sometimes signify certain sensations of the mind, which can have no existence when they are not felt, nor can exist anywhere but in a mind or sentient being; but more frequently they signify a quality in bodies, which, by the laws of nature, occasions the sensations of heat and cold in us – a quality which, though connected by custom so closely with the sensation, that we cannot, without difficulty, separate them, yet hath not the least resemblance to it, and may continue to exist when there is no sensation at all.
>
> (*Inquiry*, V.i)

The grammatical structure of our talk about sensation and perception is an additional linguistic source of confusion which may account for the ideal theorists' reification of sensations. Verbs of perception are transitive verbs, which take a noun in the accusative case. One doesn't just see, feel, hear, taste; there is always something or other that one sees, feels, and so on. After all, perception is cognitive contact with things and situations in the world. But these same verbs are used in connection with sensation, and other 'operations of the mind', and so the structure of our language requires an accusative complement, a noun or noun phrase, whether or not there is any entity distinct from the operation of the mind which the verb designates. When one suffers pain, for example, as the result of some damage to one's foot, one might well express this by saying one feels a pain in one's foot. But it does not follow from this, according to Reid, that pain is a kind of object before one's mind distinct from the feeling of it. Feeling pain is feeling a certain way; it is an illusion of grammar that may lead one to think that when one feels pain there is a mental object of which one is aware.

If it is easy to be misled, by the phenomenology of sensation and the language we use in talking about sensation, into construing an operation of the mind as an entity before the mind, it is even easier to be misled in the case of imagination and other cases in which there is no external object which is the cause of the mental representation, as *ex hypothesi* there always is in the case of perception. In fact, a great many operations of the mind do seem to involve objects distinct from the operation. And this, again, is reflected in the grammar of the verbs we use in connection with these operations.

> In most operations of the mind, there must be an object distinct from the operation itself. I cannot see, without seeing something.... I cannot remember, without remembering something. The thing remembered is past, while the remembrance of it is present; and therefore, the operation and the object of it must be distinct things.... From the general structure of language, this verb [know] requires a person ... but it requires no less a noun in the accusative case, denoting the thing known ... and to know, without having an object of knowledge, is an absurdity.
>
> (*Essays*, I.ii)

However, if one imagines an object or situation and no actual object or situation exists corresponding to the imagination, then we are tempted to posit an internal, mental object to satisfy the grammatical requirement that there be a direct object of the verb. Reid asks us to consider, for example, an artist conceiving of the picture he has not yet begun to paint.

> It is one thing to project, another to execute. A man may think for a long time what he is to do, and after all do nothing. Conceiving, as well as projecting or resolving, are what the schoolmen call *immanent* acts of the mind, which produce nothing beyond themselves. But painting is a transitive act, which produces an effect distinct from the operation, and this effect is the picture.... What is commonly called the image of the thing in the mind, is no more than the act or operation of the mind in conceiving it.... The image in the mind, therefore, is not the object of conception, nor is it any effect produced by conception as a cause. It is conception itself. That very mode of thinking which we call conception, is by another name called an image in the mind.
>
> (*Essays*, IV.i)

> But may a man who concieves a centaur say that he has a distinct image of it in his mind? ... By a distinct image in the mind, the vulgar mean a distinct conception; and it is natural to call it so, on account of an analogy between an image of a thing and a conception of it. On account of this analogy ... this operation is called imagination, and an image in the mind is only a periphrasis for imagination. But to infer from this that there is really an image in the mind, distinct from the operation of conceiving the object, is to be misled by an analogical expression.
>
> (*Essays*, IV.ii)

Imagining, conceiving, or in other words merely thinking of some object or situation, then, for Reid, is an act or operation of the mind, not a relation between the mind and some mental object or entity. In the terminology of mental representation, imagining is a manner of mentally representing, with a topic, but in no other sense need it involve positing an entity, a mental representation, to which the representing mind is related. Reifying mental representations in fact commits one to a model of the mind which leads straight to scepticism. But it is very tempting to reify mental representations; our language for talking about the mind's functioning positively encourages it. In fact, as we shall soon see, Reid's own positive account of perception appears to treat sensations as objects, albeit objects that function very differently from the mental objects of the ideal theory. Before turning to Reid's positive account of sensation and its role in perception, it would be well to attend to the second major defect Reid identifies in the theory of perception typically held by proponents of the theory of ideas.

Reid's causal theory of perception

The second crucial defect in the theory of ideas is its way of construing perceptual belief-fixation as a process of logical inference: as reasoning from premises expressing the contents of ideas of sensation to conclusions about the existence and characteristics of mind-independent things and situations.

Perception, according to Descartes and Locke, and many others who have subscribed to their model of the mind, is an inference (or judgement) we make, upon attending to ideas of sensation, to the effect that such and such material object exists whose qualities resemble, or otherwise 'conform' to, the ideas.[2] We have perceptual knowledge of the external world just in case the inference is both true and justified. As both Descartes and Locke had to admit, though, it cannot be maintained that our ideas of so-called secondary qualities, such as colour, actually resemble those qualities, because our ideas of these qualities vary in ways we do not suppose the qualities themselves vary. So the philosopher who subscribes to the theory of ideas characteristically criticizes ordinary people, the 'vulgar', 'naïve realists', who believe that colours really are qualities of objects. The philosopher knows that colours are in the mind.

The problem, of course, as the sceptic is never tired of pointing out, is actually much more serious. If our ideas are objects before

117

the mind, and are the only such objects before the mind, no inference that any quality, or any object, exists outside the mind, can ever be justified. We can have no good reason to believe that there is a world external to our minds which resembles (or otherwise 'conforms' to) our ideas. Berkeley accepted this consequence of the theory and argued that there is no extramental reality. So-called material objects are really collections of ideas (or at least, all we mean when talking about objects can be expressed by referring to ideas someone is now having or would be having if ...). Hume also traced the sceptical consequences of the theory of ideas, and agreed with the sceptic: we can have no good reason to believe in an external world, or in causal connections, or even that the future will resemble the past. The best we can do is give a psychological explanation of how we come to believe all these things and why we persist in believing them.

But if we construe perception as a causal process, in which the having of a sensation of red produces in us a belief that an extramental object is red, the problem of justifying an inference does not arise, since the particular belief that there is a red object there before one is not an inference. Of course, the second-order question of whether we have good reason to believe that the beliefs we acquire in perception are generally true, does arise. That is, we can still raise the question of whether we are justified in believing that there is an extramental world. But that is different from the question as to what justifies my belief right now that I am looking at a sheet of red paper. And that question is one Reid attempts to answer with his wholesale defence of common-sense. Since nature imposes upon us our perceptual beliefs, and we would perish if we were not caused to have these beliefs but had to reach them by reason, that in itself constitutes their justification as a class of belief.

According to Reid, we should think of sensations as functioning as *signs*, the awareness of which causes our perceptual belief, and not as bits of evidence.

> When I hear a certain sound, I conclude immediately, without reasoning, that a coach passes by. There are no premises from which this conclusion is inferred by any rules of logic. It is the effect of a principle of our nature, common to us with the brutes.
>
> (*Inquiry*, IV.i)

Although Reid uses the word 'conclude', he is not talking about the conclusion of some process of reasoning, as the rest of the passage makes clear. To conclude, as he is here using the word, is merely to come to believe. The process is causal, not rational.

118

[The sensations of smell, taste, touch] are signs by which we know and distinguish things without us; and it was fit that the variety of the signs should, in some degree, correspond to the variety of things signified by them.

(Inquiry, IV.i)

In saying that the variety of signs 'corresponds to the variety of things signified', Reid only means that the sensation of smell, for instance, is the sign of something in the world which is different from what the sensation of taste, for instance, signifies. The correspondence in question need not be cashed out in terms of resemblance, or any other sort of structural isomorphism.

We all know that a certain kind of sound suggests immediately to the mind a coach passing in the street; and not only produces the imagination, but the belief, that a coach is passing. Yet there is here no comparing of ideas, no perception of agreements or disagreements, to produce this belief: nor is there the least similitude between the sound we hear and the coach we imagine and believe to be passing.

(Inquiry, II.vii)

The sensations of smell, taste, sound and colour, are of infinitely more importance as signs or indications than they are upon their own account; like the words of a language, wherein we do not attend to the sound but to the sense.

(Inquiry, II.ix)

Sensations, however, are natural signs, not conventional ones. The relation between a particular word, say the word 'red', and the quality of objects it signifies, is conventional. Different sounds serve equally well in other languages to signify that quality. One learns what 'red' signifies when one learns the language. But one does not have to learn what the sensation of red signifies, and the connection between the sensation and the quality is not arbitrarily alterable, as is the case with conventional signs.

Reid actually distinguishes three kinds of natural signs, which differ in the connection between the sign and what it signifies and in how that connection is established in our minds. In the first class are those relationships, such as that between the appearance of smoke and the presence of fire, which are 'established by nature' and which we discover by experiencing their regular conjunction in nature and inferring the law-like connection. A second class includes the gestures, facial expressions, and other non-verbal behavioural signs of people's epistemic and desiderative states. The connection between the sign and what it signifies in these cases is established by nature, as in the first class; but we discover the connection, Reid believes, not by rational inference from experience of the connection, but by what he calls a 'natural principle', by which I think he means that our taking behaviour as a sign of thought and purpose in others develops naturally in us simply by our being members of the species. The third class of signs, in which sensations are included,

> comprehends those which, though we never before had any notion or conception of the thing signified, do suggest it, or conjure it up, as it were, by a natural kind of magic, and at once give us a conception and create a belief of it.
>
> (*Inquiry*, V.iii)

Once we recognize that we are not immediately aware of mental entities (ideas), but rather that the operation of the mind called sensation causes one to be aware of external objects via the sensations which are their natural signs, then there is nothing to prevent us from claiming that the external objects, and not the sensations, are the immediate objects of perception. What we are immediately aware of in perception are the things themselves; and our awareness of them is not mediated by the awareness of any mental object which stands for, or stands in for, the external object.

If this is Reid's view, then his analysis of perception is a version of direct realism. But in the second of the *Essays*, Reid gives an account of the role of sensation in perception which seems on the face of it to jeopardize his claim that external objects are the immediate objects of perception.

> Perception has always an immediate object; and the object of my perception, in this case, is that quality in the rose which I discern by the sense of smell. Observing that the agreeable sensation is raised when the rose is near, and ceases when it is removed, I am led, by my nature, to conclude some quality to be in the rose, which is the cause of the sensation. This quality in the rose is the object perceived; and that act of my mind by which I have the conviction and belief of this quality, is what in this case I call perception.
>
> (*Essays*, II. xvi)

Commenting on this passage in his edition of Reid's works, Sir William Hamilton voices an obvious criticism.

> This paragraph appears to be an explicit disavowal of the doctrine of an intuitive or immediate perception. If, from a certain sensible feeling, or sensation (which is itself cognizant of no

object), I am only determined by my nature to *conclude* that
there is some external quality which is the *cause* of this sensation, and if this quality, thus only known as an inference from
its effect, be the *object perceived*; then perception is not an act
immediately cognitive of any existing object, and the object
perceived is, in fact, *except as an imaginary something*,
unknown.

(Hamilton's footnote to the passage quoted above.)

Is this criticism merited? In one respect, he begs the question at
issue against Reid, by saying quite confidently that the sensation 'is
itself cognizant of no object', for Reid's account of perception
holds that being determined to conclude from the sensation that
there is a fragrant rose in front of my nose is what constitutes being
cognizant of an object. The question is doubly begged when Sir
William concludes that the object, the fragrant rose, is 'an imaginary something', since it is Reid's view that the object itself is
immediately perceived via the sensation. But Reid's 'sign theory' of
sensation does lend itself to this sort of interpretation. For instance, in the next section of the *Essays* Reid has this to say:

> Sensation taken by itself, implies neither the conception nor
> belief of any external object. It supposes a sentient being, and a
> certain manner in which that being is affected; but it supposes
> no more. Perception implies an immediate conviction and belief
> of something external – something different from both the mind
> that perceives, and from the act of perception. Things so diff-
> erent in their nature ought to be distinguished; but by our con-
> stitution, they are always united. Every different perception is
> conjoined with a sensation that is proper to it. The one is the
> sign, the other is the thing signified. They coalesce in our
> imagination. They are signified by one name, and are con-
> sidered as one simple operation.
>
> (*Essays*, II.xvii)

This is a difficult passage. The first part denies that there is any
object of any sort in sensation; there is only the sentient being and
a manner in which that being is affected. In other words, what we
call a sensation is just a *sensing*: a way in which the sentient being
is affected. But in the second part of the passage, Reid returns to
his favourite analogy, comparing perceiving with reading or listening to words. Sensations function as signs. Just as when we read
we don't attend to the marks on the page but to their sense, which
may well cause us to believe something about the world (for
example, as when we read the headline 'SUPREME COURT

QUASHES ANTI-ABORTION LAW' in the newspaper and immediately come to believe that the Supreme Court has quashed the anti-abortion law); so when we perceive, the sensation produces in us a conception of the object (as being so-and-so) and a conviction that the object is so-and-so.

However, if we are to take the analogy seriously, we must recognize that when we read, we do see the marks on the paper. These marks are objects, they exist independently of our perception of them if anything does; and whether we attend to them or not, they are presumably the immediate objects we perceive. It is hard to understand how our coming thereby to believe that the Supreme Court has quashed the law can count as our having *perceived* that the Supreme Court has quashed the law. Presumably, Reid intends us to disregard the fact that the marks on the page are objects, and to disregard the fact that we perceive the marks, if we perceive any external object, even though we don't attend to them *per se*. What we are intended to focus on is the fact that in both reading and in an ordinary case of the perception of some physical object, say, a red sheet of paper, the marks (or the sensation of red) are merely the way in which we become aware of the fact (or the red object). The marks, like the sensation of red, are *causal* intermediaries, but they are not objects on the basis of an awareness of which we infer the existence of the fact or the red sheet of paper. Nevertheless, what Reid calls our perception of the red sheet of paper is, in his words, merely a *belief* that *there is* a red sheet of paper before me, caused by the sensation of red.

Elsewhere in the *Essays*, Reid gives an account of perception and of the nature of the objects of perception which also seems to be incompatible with his direct realist convictions. Here, for instance, is his phenomenological account of perception in the chapter 'Of Perception'.

> If ... we attend to that act of our mind which we call the perception of an external object of sense, we shall find in it these three things: – *First*, Some conception or notion of the object perceived; *Secondly*, A strong and irresistible conviction and belief of its present existence; and, *Thirdly*, That this conviction and belief are immediate, and not the effect of reasoning.
>
> (*Essays*, II.v)

By a conception or notion of the object, Reid means some mental description or characterization of it: what it is, what its properties are, and so on. These conceptions may be more or less distinct, depending upon the conditions of observation, the conditions of the perceiver's perceptual system, and so on. The notion or conception is not an object of which we are aware; it is not a Cartesian idea or sense-datum. Its identity is perhaps best conceived as propositional, not phenomenal. For instance, our notion of an object will be influenced by other things we know or believe, which we are not perceiving at the moment. Memory thus affects what notion we have of an object, and indeed Reid speaks of notions of an object we may form from memory or imagination, at times we are not perceiving it.

To this 'first person' phenomenological account (i.e., an account of what it is like to perceive something), we can add the 'third person' causal account of perception Reid gave us in his analysis of sensations, to arrive at the following view. Physical objects in our environment act on our sense organs to produce sensations (i.e., acts of sensing), to which we do not generally attend, though sensing is a form of conscious awareness. Our nature is so constituted that the sensation immediately causes us to form a notion (conception) of the object that caused the sensation, and also causes us to form a belief in the present existence of the object 'answering to' the notion we have formed of it. The whole process is causal, not rational. But how can Reid maintain that coming to have a belief, as a result of having a sensation caused by the object, to the effect that there is an object at present existing corresponding to my conception, can possibly count as a case of immediate or direct perception of that object, even if it does exist, and even if it does really answer to my conception of it?

According to his conception of sensation, sensations are not objects before the mind. Here Reid is on the right track, in contrast to the Cartesian conception. But if sensations are operations of the mind which function as signs, they can't bring us into immediate cognitive contact with objects; they can merely cause us to conceive of something and believe that it exists. When I read the words 'Lucia is a tall woman with wavy black hair', I will perhaps conceive of Lucia and believe that she is tall and has wavy black hair. That is a kind of cognitive contact with Lucia, but it is hardly immediate. It is mediated by reading the words. But when I see the tall, wavy-black-haired Lucia and thereby come to believe that she is tall and has wavy black hair, Reid wants to say that the cognitive contact with Lucia and her wavy black hair is immediate and direct.

What Reid should have said about the role of sensation in perception was something like the following: objects in the world cause sensations in us, which are operations of the mind by which we represent the objects as having certain qualities. The sensations are, that is, constitute, our immediate awareness, our unmediated cognitive contact, with the object. They don't merely suggest the conception of the object and cause the belief in it. Reid almost put this view together, but his preoccupation with signs stood in his way.

Primary and secondary qualities

Reid's fifth principle of contingent truths states: 'Those things do really exist which we distinctly perceive with our senses, and are what we perceive them to be.' Yet his account of the distinction between our sensations of the qualities of objects and the qualities of which they are the sensations appears at first glance to commit him to a view inconsistent with the realism expressed in the fifth principle. For Reid, along with Descartes and Locke, distinguishes between primary and secondary qualities, and maintains, also in agreement with them, that our sensations of primary qualities inform us what those qualities are in themselves, whereas our sensations of secondary qualities do not.

> Our senses give us a direct and a distinct notion of the primary qualities, and inform us what they are in themselves. But of the secondary qualities, our senses give us only a relative and obscure notion. They inform us only, that they are qualities that affect us in a certain manner – that is, produce in us a certain sensation; but as to what they are in themselves, our senses leave us in the dark.
>
> (*Essays*, II.xvii)

A relative notion of something is a notion of it only as an unknown cause of a known effect. Reid mentions as an example our notion of gravity as the unknown cause of the tendency of bodies to move towards the earth, whereas our notion of gravity as that tendency itself is not a relative notion (*Essays*, II. xvii).

> The notion we have of primary qualities is direct, and not relative only. A relative notion of a thing is, strictly speaking, no notion of the thing at all, but only of some relation which it bears to something else.
>
> (*Essays*, II.xvi)

Reid hastens to point out that the common person, unversed in theory, is confused concerning the distinction between primary and secondary qualities, but is not actually mistaken.

> It is not to be expected that [the vulgar] should make distinc-

tions which have no connection with the common affairs of life;
they do not ... distinguish the primary from the secondary
qualities, but speak of both as being equally qualities of the
external object.... Of the secondary, their notions are ...
confused and indistinct, rather than erroneous.

(*Essays*, II.xvii)

Can Reid have it both ways? It would seem that either he must
maintain that the principles of common sense are correct, in which
case it is correct to believe that external objects really do have
those qualities they are perceived as having (i.e., which we immediately are caused to believe them to have as a result of the
sensations caused in us by their effect on our sense organs); or he
must maintain that external objects do not really have some of the
qualities we perceive them as having. Is red, for example, really a
quality of external objects or is it not? His answer is that red really
is a quality of external objects, just as we believe; namely, it is the
(unknown) quality that causes us to have sensations of red, and
thence to conceive of the object as red, and thence to believe that
there is a red object before us. This answer anticipates Kripke's
(1972) realist account of the reference of colour words. Kripke
writes:

Yellowness is not a dispositional property, although it is related
to a disposition. Philosophers have often, for want of any other
theory of the meaning of the term 'yellow', been inclined to
regard it as expressing a dispositional property. At the same
time, they have been much bothered by the 'gut feeling' that
yellowness is a manifest property, just as much 'right out there'
as hardness or spherical shape. The proper account, on the
present conception ... is that the reference of 'yellowness' is fixed
by the description 'that (manifest) property of objects which
causes them, under normal circumstances, to be seen as yellow
(i.e. to be sensed by certain visual impressions)'. 'Yellow' ...
does not *mean* 'tends to produce such and such a sensation'; if
we had different neural structures, if atmospheric conditions
had been different, if we had been blind, and so on, yellow
objects would have done no such thing.

(Kripke 1972: 354)

But to take this way out of the difficulty, Reid has to say that red
really is this unknown quality of which we have only a relative
notion. And this is just what he does say. This is all he means by
saying that our sensations of red do not 'inform us' what the quality
is 'in itself'.

125

> The vulgar apply the name of colour to that quality of bodies
> which excites in us what philosophers call *the idea of colour*....
> Hence it appears, that, when philosophers affirm that colour is
> not in bodies, but in the mind, and the vulgar affirm that colour
> is not in the mind, but is a quality of bodies, there is no
> difference between them about things, but only about the
> meaning of a word.
>
> (*Inquiry*, VI.v)

The difficulty disappears, that is to say, when we recognize that
the question, 'Is it really red?' is not the same as the question, 'Is it
really like our sensation of it?' A negative answer to the latter
question is only inconsistent with a positive answer to the former
within the context of a theory according to which the question of
the reality of secondary qualities reduces to the question of
whether the qualities resemble the ideas, for on such a theory,
ideas are objects which represent in the same way that images or
pictures are thought to represent, by resemblance. So Reid can
deny that the qualities are like the sensations without retreating
from realism with respect to the qualities.

In fact, the question, 'What are qualities of objects really like in
and of themselves?' is a perfectly senseless question. It is the
question of what they look like, or sound like, and so on, when no
one is looking at them, hearing them, and so on, or it is the
question of how they would appear to a perceiver not constrained
by the point of view constituted by having sense organs, being
located in a certain position in relation to the object, and so on.
But the question, 'Is the object red in and of itself?' is no different
from the question, 'Is the object really round in and of itself?' In
both cases, the answer is 'yes'. Reid goes astray in thinking that our
senses 'inform us' in a more excellent manner about the so-called
primary qualities than they do about the secondary qualities. His
inconsistency is in maintaining that primary qualities are any different from secondary qualities in this respect. All our 'notions' of
the qualities of objects are, in his terminology, relative.

Reid could, however, maintain with perfect consistency that
'things are as we perceive them to be'. He could argue as follows:
light reflecting from the object into our eyes causes in us a sensation of red, which causes us to believe that the object is red. If the
causal process is 'normal', we are therein directly perceiving a red
object, and we are therein directly perceiving it to be red. Common sense has no clear conception of what redness is, i.e., what it
is in the physical nature of the object that causes it to produce
sensations of red in us under appropriate conditions. Nor does

126

common sense have a clear idea of precisely what a normal causal process in perception is.[3] It is the business of science (which Reid included under the rubric 'philosophy') to investigate this, just as it is the business of science, and not common sense, to specify what constitutes a normal causal process. But it was open to Reid to claim that the object really is red if it is such that under the appropriate conditions it causes sensations of red in us. By insisting that our 'notion' of the quality redness is only relative and obscure, and does not inform us what redness is in itself, Reid gave more comfort to the opponents of common-sense realism than he needed to.

It was Reid's achievement to identify the foundations of the sceptical challenge to common-sense realism in the model of the mind that Hume inherited from Descartes via Locke and Berkeley. His critique of the Cartesian model is both penetrating and subtle, though in his own positive account he fell prey to the same 'pathological' tendency to construe sensations in a way that makes it impossible to hold that in perception we are directly aware of objects in the world themselves.

7

G. E. Moore: direct realism and common sense

The most famous defender of common sense in the twentieth century was G. E. Moore. In his paper 'A Defence of Common Sense' (*DCS*), he argued that 'the common sense view of the world is, in certain fundamental features, *wholly* true' (*DCS*: 44).[1] He acknowledged that the expression 'common sense' has not been used in a very precise way by philosophers, and he allowed for the possibility that there may be propositions properly included in the common-sense view of the world which are not true, 'and which deserve to be mentioned with the contempt with which some philosophers speak of "common-sense beliefs" ' (*DCS*: 45).

It is not at all easy to determine exactly what Moore meant when he talked of the common-sense view of the world. Neither in this paper, nor elsewhere in his writings, did Moore attempt to give a general characterization of the common-sense view. More importantly, he did not anywhere attempt to give a general characterization of the 'certain fundamental features' of the common-sense view which are, he claimed, wholly true. His only method of identifying the common-sense view, or those fundamental features of it that he is concerned to defend, was simply to list various propositions expressing one or more of these features.

It will be convenient to use the label 'common-sense proposition' for any proposition Moore identified as expressing one or more fundamental features of the common-sense view. The problem of determining exactly what constitutes the fundamental part of the common-sense view of the world Moore wished to defend then becomes the problem of determining the conditions any proposition must satisfy in order to qualify as a common-sense proposition.

The long list of common-sense propositions Moore provides near the beginning of 'A Defence of Common Sense' is very heterogeneous. Here are some examples:

1. There exists at present a living human body, which is *my* body.

2. This body was born at a certain time in the past, and has existed continuously ever since.

3. Ever since it was born, it has been either in contact with or not far from the surface of the earth.

4. Among the things which have ... formed part of its environment ... there have been large numbers of other living human bodies.

5. The earth had existed ... for many years before my body was born.

6. I am a human being, and I have ... had many different experiences.

7. I have often perceived both my own body and other things which form part of its environment.

8. I have not only perceived things ... but I have also observed facts about them.

9. I have been aware of other facts, which I was not at the time observing, such as ... the fact that my body existed yesterday.

(*DCS*: 35–6)

Each of them Moore considers to be a truism 'which (in my own opinion) I know with certainty to be true'. The only unifying element in the list is that each proposition in some way makes reference to G. E. Moore: to his body and its environment, or to his experiences. But lest we conclude that all common-sense propositions are about G. E. Moore (which would constitute a curious interpretation of 'the fundamental features of the common-sense view of the world'), Moore adds that there is another common-sense proposition 'which (in my own opinion) I know with certainty to be true': namely, that there are very many other human beings besides himself, who have bodies, have lived upon the earth, and had experiences of the sort Moore has had, each of whom knows, or has known, with regard to himself or herself and his or her body, propositions corresponding to those Moore listed as knowing with regard to himself and his body.

This addition increases the distribution of what Moore took to be common-sense propositions, but it hardly provides a general criterion for identifying them. All such propositions are propositions which a person does or could assert with reference to his or her own body, experiences, or physical environment. It is hardly likely, however, that Moore wished to claim that every such proposition is a common-sense proposition, for the very good reason that he held that all common-sense propositions are known with certainty to be true; but it is obvious that many propositions people assert in which reference is made to their bodies, experiences, or physical environment are not only not known with certainty to be true, but are quite plainly false.

Although Moore did not give a general characterization, in 'A Defence of Common Sense' or anywhere else, of the common-sense view of the world, in 'Some Judgments of Perception' (*SJP*),[2] he did give a general characterization of one prominent type of proposition included on the above list. These are propositions, such as numbers 7 and 8, which Moore called 'judgments of perception'. Perhaps by attending closely to what Moore had to say about judgements of perception in that paper we can get a better idea of what it is about these propositions that makes them part of the common-sense view of the world; and we may also thereby get a better idea of the general strategy behind his defence of common sense.

Judgements of perception

Moore first identifies a kind of judgement that we all very commonly make.

> The kind of judgments I mean are those which we make when, with regard to something we are seeing, we judge such things as 'That is an inkstand', 'That is a table cloth', 'That is a door', etc., etc.; or when, with regard to something which we are feeling with our hands, we judge such things as 'This is a cloth', 'This is a finger', 'This is a coin', etc. etc.
>
> (*SJP*: 220)

Moore singled out this kind of judgement for special attention because

> judgments of this kind would, I think, commonly and rightly, be taken to be judgments, the truth of which involves the existence of material things or physical objects. If I am right in judging that this is an inkstand, it follows that there is at least one inkstand in the Universe; and if there is an inkstand in the Universe, it follows that there is in it at least one material thing or physical object.
>
> (*SJP*: 221)

Each judgement of this sort is, of course, a judgement expressing common-sense realism, the metaphysical component of common sense. Moore did not use the label 'realism' in connection with these judgements, however, for reasons that will become apparent. Nor did he wish to call all judgements of this kind judgements of perception. He wished to reserve this technical term to denote a sub-class of this kind of judgement having certain special features. This sub-class he identified as follows:

> In every case in which I judge, with regard to something which I am seeing or feeling with my hands, that it is a so-and-so, simply because I do perceive, by sight or touch that it is in fact of that kind, we can, I think, fairly say that the judgment in question is a judgment of perception. And enormous numbers of judgments of the kind I mean are, quite plainly, judgments of perception in this sense. They are not *all*, for the simple reason that some of them are mistaken. I may, for instance, judge, with regard to an animal which I see at a distance, that it is a sheep, when in fact it is a pig. And here my judgment is certainly not due to the fact that I see it to be a sheep, since I cannot possibly see a thing to be a sheep unless it is one. It, therefore, is *not* a judgment of perception in this sense. And moreover, even where such a judgment is true, it may not always be a judgment of perception, for the reason that, whereas I only see the thing in question, the kind of thing which I judge it to be is of such a nature, that it is impossible for anyone, by sight alone, to perceive anything to be of that kind.
>
> (*SJP*: 225–6)

According to Moore, then, a judgement is a judgement of perception if and only if: (1) it is, or could be, expressed in a proposition of the form 'that is a so-and-so', where the term 'so-and-so' denotes a kind of physical object, and (2) it is based on perceiving that the thing in question is a so-and-so. Clearly, since perceiving that a is b logically entails that a is b, we can see why Moore said that all judgements of perception without exception are true. Furthermore, since Moore held that perceiving that a is b is a form of knowing that a is b, or at least expresses such knowledge, then every judgement of perception is not only true but known to be true. Thus, according to Moore, it is part of the common-sense view of the world that there *are* judgements of perception, in the strict sense of 'judgement of perception' just defined.

What did Moore think the justification is for claiming that we know that there are judgements of perception, or that on any particular occasion we are in a position to know that we are judging that something is an inkstand on the basis of perceiving that it is one? This question should not be confused with the somewhat different set of questions that Moore did consider and dispose of in 'A Defence of Common Sense'. There he imagined his opponent either denying that common-sense propositions as a class are true, or alternatively, of denying that we can know that any of them are true. Moore argued that any philosopher who denies that the common-sense view of the world is true is guilty of self-refutation, for if the common-sense view is false, then there are not now, and never have been, any philosophers, and therefore no philosopher could ever deny that any common-sense proposition is true. If any philosopher exists and denies the truth of the common-sense view of the world, then the common-sense view is true and that philosopher is surely wrong.

> For when I speak of 'philosophers' I mean, of course (as we all do), exclusively philosophers who have been human beings, with human bodies that have lived upon the earth, and who have at different times had many different experiences.
>
> (*DCS*: 40)

Now some philosophers, says Moore, are prepared to admit that all common-sense propositions *may* be true, but they claim that, with regard to those common-sense propositions which assert the existence of material things or of selves other than one's own self, no one can *know* that any such proposition is true. Moore's reply to these philosophers was that what they say is not self-refuting but actually self-contradictory, since anyone who asserts that no one can know whether any such proposition is true, 'is saying "There have been many other beings besides myself, and none of them (including myself) has ever known of the existence of other human beings" ' (*DCS*: 43). Moore thought that this position is self-contradictory because, unlike the first view, it makes a claim about human knowledge, and therefore actually asserts the existence of human beings, namely, beings other than oneself, with bodies, who have lived upon the earth, had many different experiences, and so on.

These audacious arguments do not, I think, have a great deal of force against the careful sceptic concerning common sense. A logically naïve but hyperbolic solipsist might well believe, or at least believe that she believes, that there are no human beings with bodies who have lived on the earth and had experiences; for she might believe that only the present conscious experience exists, with its apparent memories of previous experiences, apparent perceptions of bodies, and so on. Believing (or believing she believes) this, she might be rash enough to audibly assert as much in someone else's presence with the intention of convincing them, or write it down for publication. That would certainly be self-refuting. A more sophisticated sceptic regarding common sense would argue, as for instance Hume did, that our common-sense belief that we have bodies, and that we and others live upon the earth, includes believing that our bodies, other so-called material objects, and the earth itself have a continuous existence independent of our own or anyone else's experiences. And if the sceptic were to deny this feature of common sense (as Hume most certainly did not), she would not thereby refute herself.

Now it was Moore's view that what I have called the more sophisticated sceptic is not really denying the *truth* of any common-sense proposition. She is only disputing one *analysis* of what the propositions of common sense mean. If the sophisticated sceptic is prepared to assert that she does have a body, does live on the earth, and so on, then she has no quarrel with common sense, in Moore's view, even though she should deny that anything at all exists independently of experience. Since I shall be taking up Moore's views on the distinction between the truth of common-sense beliefs and their analysis later in the present chapter, I shall say no more in criticism of Moore's first argument here.

Moore's second argument is very weak. An epistemological sceptic foolish enough to formulate his view in the form of words that Moore puts in his mouth would indeed be guilty of self-contradiction. But a more careful epistemological sceptic might, like Hume, formulate a general view about the nature and source of knowledge, and then go on to argue, as Hume did, that the knowledge claims people actually make concerning common-sense propositions cannot be justified as constituting genuine knowledge. Such a sceptic might have seriously defective views about what knowledge is, or about its legitimate source(s); but he cannot be justly accused of self-contradiction in the act of arguing for them.

Moore did, however, have another argument in defence of the common-sense view, or at least in defence of some of the propositions of common sense. This is the argument Moore gives in 'Some Judgments of Perception' as a justification for claiming that he does know with certainty that judgements of perception are true.[3]

> Some philosophers seem to me to have denied that we ever do
> in fact know such things as these, and others not only that we
> ever know them but also that they are ever true. And if, in fact,
> I never do know such a thing, or if it is never true, it will, of
> course, follow that I never perceive such a thing; since I
> certainly cannot in this sense perceive anything whatever,
> unless I both know it and it is true. But it seems to me a
> sufficient refutation of such views as these, simply to point to
> cases in which we do know such things. This, after all, you
> know, really is a finger: there is no doubt about it: I know it,

and you all know it. And I think we may safely challenge any philosopher to bring any argument in favour either of the proposition that we do not know it, or of the proposition that it is not true, which does not at some point, rest upon some premiss which is, beyond comparison, less certain than is the proposition which it is designed to attack. The questions whether we do ever know such things as these, and whether there are any material things, seem to me, therefore, to be questions which there is no need to take seriously: they are questions which it is quite easy to answer, with certainty, in the affirmative.

(*SJP*: 227–8)

In this argument, which echoes the first of Reid's arguments in defence of common sense discussed in the previous chapter, Moore makes implicit use of the concept of *subjective probability*, or the degree of confidence we may have towards the propositions we entertain. In our everyday lives, we are more confident of the truth of some propositions than of others. These degrees of confidence can be regarded as indices of subjective probability, ranging between 1 (subjective certainty of the truth of the proposition) and 0 (subjective certainty of the negation of the proposition). For the most part, our confidence in the propositions we entertain amounts to less than 1 and more than 0. This is true of most of the propositions we would say that we believe. Gentle reader, most likely you believe that you will be alive tomorrow; but such is our awareness of the fragility of human life, most likely you are not certain of it.

Moore's view, as expressed in the passage just quoted, is that our degree of confidence in common-sense propositions is so great, amounting in fact to subjective certainty, that any argument that can be brought forward to challenge our claim to know that a common-sense proposition is true, in particular that some judgement of perception such as 'This is a hand' is true, will at some point have to make use of a proposition as a premiss which is less certain, which has lower subjective probability, than the proposition that is being challenged.

The subjective certainty of the propositions of common sense is indeed the real foundation of Moore's defence in 'A Defence of Common Sense'. On the very first page Moore announces that he will defend a set of propositions 'every one of which (in my own opinion) I know with certainty to be true'. And throughout the paper, whenever Moore wishes to claim that he knows with certainty some particular common-sense proposition, he always prefaces it by saying '(in my own opinion), I know with certainty' such-and-such. Moore was a very careful writer. If he had meant to claim boldly that something was known with certainty to be true, he would have said so *sans phrase*. What then is the force of the qualifying parenthetical phrase?

The logic of the verb 'know' is such that for any proposition *p* and any subject *s*, the truth of the statement '*S* knows that *p*' entails the truth of *p*. Thus I cannot say without absurdity, 'I know *p*, but perhaps *p* is false.' Now suppose Moore had said of each of the propositions on his list, 'I know with certainty that this proposition is true.' He would thereby have begged the question in favour of the truth of 'the fundamental features' of the common-sense view of the world. In that case, his defence of common sense would be no defence at all, but merely a dogmatic assertion. In order to be in a position to mount a defence of common sense, therefore, Moore had to restrict himself to claiming '(in my own opinion), I know with certainty' the truth of each and every common-sense proposition.

By qualifying his knowledge claim in this way, Moore expresses the view that every common-sense proposition is subjectively certain. Moore is psychologically convinced that he knows each such proposition to be true. He gives no credence at all to the negation of any common-sense proposition. But he claims more than this. By adding to his list of common-sense propositions those expressing common-sense knowledge on the part of other people, Moore expresses his subjective certainty that other people are also subjectively certain of propositions corresponding to the ones Moore is subjectively certain he knows. The fact that these propositions are subjectively certain for Moore, and the fact that he is subjectively certain that they are subjectively certain for others as well, constitutes the main bulwark of his defence of the propositions of common sense.

Since the statement '(In my own opinion), I know that *p* is true' does not entail that *p* is true, Moore avoids the charge of begging the question from the very beginning. But although we can acknowledge that Moore has not begged the question in favour of common sense, we still have to ask quite bluntly: well, what *is* the force of Moore's defence if it comes down to arguing that the propositions of common sense are subjectively certain, that Moore cannot give any credence to the possibility of their being false, nor can he give any credence to the idea that anyone else can give credence to this possibility; whereas any argument designed to show that these propositions are false, or are not known to be true, will contain at least one premiss which is considerably less than subjectively certain?

In the end, I think his argument does not have much force, but it will require a fairly detailed examination of Moore's analysis of judgements of perception to see that this is so. What his argument amounts to is this. Since each proposition of common-sense, according to Moore, is not only subjectively certain for Moore, but, if he is right, a corresponding proposition is subjectively certain for each of us; and since, according to Moore, any argument to the effect that we do not know that a common-sense proposition is true will rest at some point on a premiss that is less subjectively certain than the common-sense proposition itself, then the only avenue open to someone who would attempt to show that the common-sense propositions are false, or not known to be true, is to bring forward a sceptical argument which does not at any point rest on a premiss or premisses less certain than the proposition under attack. But to do that would be to show that the propositions of common sense (which are subjectively certain) either form an inconsistent set, or are incompatible with some other subjectively certain proposition(s). That is, what the sceptic would have to do is construct a valid argument every premiss of which is subjectively certain, but which has as its conclusion the negation of some important class of common-sense propositions, or concludes with the assertion that we cannot know that some important class of common-sense propositions is true.

However, in saying that 'we may safely challenge' any philosopher to bring forward such an argument, Moore expressed his complete confidence that no such argument can be constructed. Why? Because Moore was subjectively certain that each common-sense proposition is known to be true, and for that very reason no credence can be given by him to the possibility that the common-sense view of the world is inconsistent. Therefore, the ultimate ground of Moore's defence of common sense is the claim that either common sense is inconsistent or we are completely justified in asserting that we know with certainty that it is true.

Now there actually is a famous sceptical argument, the 'argument from illusion', which in at least some of its versions is an attempt to show that the common-sense view of the world is indeed inconsistent. Indeed, we have already encountered it in Chapters 5 and 6. However, Moore took the view that the argument from illusion is not really an argument against the common-sense view itself, but against a particular theory concerning the *analysis* of those common-sense propositions Moore called judgements of perception. Thus, even if the argument from illusion succeeds, it would not thereby show that the common-sense view is inconsistent, in Moore's opinion. It would merely show that one suggested analysis of a certain type of common-sense proposition cannot be consistently maintained.

Direct realism and the argument from illusion

Since Moore defends common sense, and since, as we have seen, included in the common-sense view are judgements of perception, among which are judgements such as 'This is a hand', said on the basis of perceiving that this is a hand, one might naturally expect that Moore would consider the philosophical position known as direct realism to be a component of the common-sense view of the world, as Reid clearly did. Direct realism is the view that we are in immediate cognitive contact in perception with objects in the world which exist independently of our perception of them and thought about them, and which have the 'qualities' we perceive them as having. But Moore did not think that a commitment to direct realism is a component of common sense. Direct realism and its philosophical rivals are, according to Moore, competing views on the correct analysis of common-sense propositions.

According to Moore, one can be convinced that a judgement of perception is true, and still dispute whether direct realism is true. Consequently, direct realism is not entailed by the truth of the common-sense view of the world, but rather is involved in the question of its correct analysis. The analysis of a proposition reveals what that proposition means, in a sense of 'means' that Moore never really succeeded in making clear. In one sense we all know what common-sense propositions mean. That is, when we are confronted with a common-sense proposition, we have no difficulty at all in understanding it. We know, in that sense, what it means. And yet there's another sense in which, perhaps, we do not know what common-sense propositions mean. As Moore sometimes put it: although we know that a particular common-sense proposition, say a judgement of perception, is true, yet we may not know precisely what it is that's involved in our knowing that it's true.

Perhaps what Moore had in mind by a philosophical analysis is something like this. A philosophical analysis of the meaning of a common-sense proposition, or of any other proposition, is nothing other than a detailed specification of the truth conditions of that proposition. Such an analysis might have the form: 'I see an ink-stand' is true, if and only if .... One then specifies the conditions under which the sentence is true. Now in one sense we already know the truth conditions of 'This is my hand' or 'I see an inkstand', for we know the boring but not trivial fact that for any proposition *p*, *p* is true if and only if *p* is the case. Furthermore, since the proposition to be analysed is a common-sense proposition, we already know, according to Moore, that the truth conditions, whatever they are, *are* satisfied. We know that *p* is the case. But we may not know in each of these cases what in turn has to be the case in order for *p* to be the case. That is, we might not know what the necessary and sufficient conditions are which have to be satisfied in order for it to be the case that I see an inkstand, or for it to be the case that the referent of the demonstrative 'this' is indeed my hand. If we look at it this way, then, what Moore attempts to do in the latter part of 'A Defence of Common Sense', and throughout 'Some Judgments of Perception' and many other works, is to discuss the question of how we might specify the detailed truth conditions for one or another common-sense proposition.

Moore did claim to know one essential component of the analysis of any judgement of perception, but he never thought he was successful in discovering the complete analysis of such propositions. What he claimed to know with certainty was that any satisfactory analysis of any judgement of perception must make reference to a thing which we *directly apprehend* whenever we perceive any item in our physical environment. Moore usually used the technical term 'sense-datum' to refer to this posited item. Thus, according to Moore, some 'sense-datum statement' is a necessary constituent of the analysis of any judgement of perception. For instance, part of the analysis of 'I see my hand' would be this: 'I directly apprehend this sense-datum.' But with regard to any subsequent condition(s) Moore confessed that he had great difficulty.

Moore's usual method of specifying the reference of the term 'sense-datum' was quasi-ostensive. He would invite the reader to attend to certain phenomenologically, (i.e., introspectively) salient features of a typical judgement of perception. His description of these features would, he hoped, enable one to discover for oneself what Moore meant by the technical term 'sense-datum', by means of discovering a sense-datum one is oneself aware of in the perceptual situation. I shall discuss two examples of Moore's method of introducing the term 'sense-datum'. The first is from 'Some Judgments of Perception', and the second is from 'A Defence of Common Sense'.

In all cases in which I make a judgment of this sort [that is, a judgment of perception], I have no difficulty whatever in picking out a thing which is, quite plainly, in a sense in which nothing else is, *the* thing about which I am making my judgment; and yet, though this thing is *the* thing about which I am judging, I am, quite certainly, *not*, in general, judging with regard to it, that *it* is a thing of that kind for which the term, which seems to express the predicate of my judgment, is a name. Thus when I judge, as now, that this is an inkstand, I have no difficulty whatever in picking out, from what, if you like, you can call my total field of presentation at the moment, an object, which is undoubtedly, in a sense in which nothing else is, *the* object about which I am making this judgment; and yet it seems to me quite certain that of *this* object I am not judging that it is a whole inkstand.

(*SJP*: 229)

This is a particularly labyrinthine passage, even by Moore's standards. He first claims that in every judgement of perception he, and presumably anyone else suitably instructed in what to attend to, can easily identify *the* thing which is the ultimate subject of the judgement. In the judgement 'That is an inkstand', for instance, this item is the real or ultimate referent of the demonstrative pronoun 'that'. Later he says that we may define the technical term 'sense-datum' by saying that sense-data are 'the sorts of things, *about* which such judgments as these always seem to be made: the sorts of things which seem to be the real or ultimate subjects of all such judgments' (*SJP*: 231–2). The technique is phenomenological in that one merely has to attend to one's state of consciousness when making a judgement of perception in order to identify, within one's 'total field of presentation', that item one intends to denote by the use of the demonstrative pronoun. The technique is virtually identical to Descartes's phenomenological method for identifying his *ideas*, though of course not all Cartesian ideas are sensory phenomena. Moorean sense-data are rather like Lockean *ideas of sensation*.

It should be clear that the 'field of presentation' to which Moore refers is itself specified purely phenomenologically. It is everything present to sensory consciousness when one attends introspectively to one's state of consciousness in making a judgement of perception. It would be question-begging to identify the field of presentation with some region of the perceiver's physical environment, at this stage of the analysis. For clearly, whether or not the field of presentation is identical with some region of the perceiver's environment is not a matter the perceiver can settle phenomenologically, or introspectively, for reasons with which we have been familiar since Descartes. What has not been as readily recognized by philosophers, or certainly not recognized by Descartes, Locke, Berkeley, or Hume, is the fact that it would be equally question-begging to assert that the field of presentation is *not* a region of the perceiver's physical environment. For this also cannot be determined by the perceiver on purely phenomenological grounds.

Therefore, the sense-datum, the 'presented object', has an as yet undetermined ontological status. Although Moore is convinced that there is a presented object – he thinks it is phenomenologically obvious that he is picking out *something* as the subject of his judgement – its ontological status must remain undetermined, at least until further questions are answered.

It is important to distinguish Moore's phenomenological technique for introducing the term 'sense-datum' into the analysis of judgements of perception from another technique much favoured by philosophers who have made use of the technical term 'sense-datum'. This other technique is to posit sense-data as special, non-physical entities after allegedly demonstrating, usually via some version of the argument from illusion, that we cannot consistently maintain that physical objects really have certain properties they experientially appear to have. For example, the partially immersed oar appears bent, but it isn't really bent. However, this argument runs, *something bent* is immediately present in my field of presentation. The sense-datum is then introduced as the 'really bent' item in the perceptual situation. This technique does commit anyone who employs it to a decision concerning the ontological status of sense-data: namely, the decision to deny that sense-data can possibly be identical with physical objects or parts of their surfaces. Thus this technique rules out a direct-realist analysis of perception from the very beginning, whereas Moore's phenomenological technique specifically intended to leave open the direct-realist hypothesis.

Moore also makes another claim on phenomenological grounds in the passage under discussion. He is not, he says, 'in general', judging the sense-datum – the ultimate referent of 'that' in the judgement 'That is an inkstand' – to be itself a member of the class of inkstands. His ground for this seemingly bizarre claim is that the expression 'inkstand' denotes a class of objects each of which has properties (for example, bottoms, insides) that the sense-datum is not *presented* as having. He would, he thinks, be making a kind of inferential leap if he were to judge that the *presented item* has an inside, or a bottom. So he specifically refrains from judging that the sense-datum is a whole inkstand, but at most judges that it is *part of the surface* of one.

The general principle Moore seems to be employing here is that one shouldn't judge that what one sees is in fact a whole x (e.g., inkstand, hand) unless one sees the whole of it. Now perhaps we should exercise such scrupulous restraint in our ordinary judgements of perception. But as a plain matter of phenomenological fact, we don't. Usually, when we think we have seen a large enough or a significant enough portion of some familiar object, we judge that what we see is the object itself, for in everyday life seeing largish or significant portions of things is what counts as seeing those things. So if I were honestly to ask myself whether I am judging that the referent of 'that' in my present judgement 'That is a hand', is itself a member of the class of hands, I would have to answer in the affirmative. And I think Moore would also have to answer in the affirmative if he were investigating the phenomenology of an ordinary judgement of perception and not engaging in philosophical debate. One might be wrong in judging that the referent of 'that' *is* my hand, but for better or worse, that is what is judged in common-sense judgements of perception. One would be prepared to admit, of course, that at the very moment one actually sees only part of the hand's surface; but that does not affect the judgement one actually makes: namely, in 'That is a hand', one is judging the referent of 'that' to be one's hand.

Moore's method of specifying the reference of the term 'sense-datum' in 'A Defence of Common Sense' is also phenomenological, and is entirely consistent with the method used in the earlier paper.

> In order to point out to the reader what sorts of things I mean by sense-data, I need only ask him to look at his own right hand. If he does this he will be able to pick out something (and, unless he is seeing double, *only* one thing) with regard to which he will see that it is, at first sight, a natural view to take that the thing is identical, not, indeed, with his whole right hand, but with that part of its surface which he is actually seeing, but will also (on a little reflection) be able to see that it is doubtful whether it can be identical with the part of the surface of his hand in question. Things *of the sort* (in a certain respect) of which this thing is, which he sees in looking at his hand, and with regard to which he can understand how some philosophers should have supposed it to *be* the part of the surface of his hand which he is seeing, while others have supposed that it can't be, are what I mean by 'sense-data'. I therefore define the term in

such a way that it is an open question whether the sense-datum which I now see in looking at my hand and which is a sense-datum of my hand is or is not identical with that part of its surface I am now actually seeing.

(*DCS*: 54–5)

Thus we see that Moore used the expression 'sense-datum' simply to *denote* that which is the ultimate subject of a judgement of perception, whatever that might be (that is, whatever the nature of sense-data might turn out to be on further investigation). The nature of sense-data, apart from their being that which we are immediately aware of, or the ultimate subjects of judgements of perception, was not specified by Moore, for the very good reason that Moore did not claim to know, or even to have a clear notion of, what sense-data really are apart from their being the ultimate referents of 'that' in judgements of perception of the form 'That is a so-and-so.'

Having identified sense-data in what he thinks is an ontologically neutral way, Moore is able to formulate the central question concerning the analysis of judgements of perception without begging the question for or against any theory, including direct realism. Since genuine judgements of perception are all true and all entail the existence of physical objects, and since all such judgements have as their ultimate subject a sense-datum, every judgement of perception is of the form: this sense-datum stands in the relation R to the physical object O. The central question asks for the correct substituend for R.

By attending carefully to our judgements of perception as we make them, what can we discover about the relation R? For most of his career, Moore thought that there were only two likely candidates. One candidate is identity: the view that the sense-datum is (and is judged to be) identical with a part of the surface of the physical object perceived. In 1918, Moore confessed that he was inclined towards this view. Clearly, if it is correct, then some version of direct realism is the correct analysis of judgements of perception. On the other hand, if there is some insuperable objection to this view, then no version of direct realism can possibly be true. The other leading candidate, in Moore's opinion, is some form of phenomenalism, which Moore referred to in 1918 by the label 'a view of the Mill–Russell type'. Mill (1872) had expressed the view that what we call physical objects are actually just 'permanent possibilities of sensation'. Russell (1917) had recommended that we think of physical objects not as entities the existence of which we infer from the evidence of sense-data, but rather as 'logical constructs' out of sense-data themselves. In the view of both philosophers, all the empirical content of judgements of perception can be expressed by a series of conditional statements about what sense-data would be directly apprehended if certain conditions were to obtain, these conditions also being expressed in terms of sense-data.

Although inclined towards direct realism, Moore is aware of a seemingly fatal objection to it. The objection relies in part on a version of Leibniz's law of the identity of indiscernibles, and in part on an ontological claim about the nature of sense-data. If the presented object (the sense-datum) is identical with this part of the surface of the physical object, then anything which is true of this part of the surface of the physical object must be true of this sense-datum, and vice versa. But, says Moore, if on each of two occasions I perceive the same part of the same physical object, it may happen that I will judge that the part of the surface in question is not perceptibly different on the second occasion from on the first; but I may judge with equal certainty that the presented object, the sense-datum, *is* perceptibly different on the second occasion.

> If I am looking at it [i.e., a coin] from a sufficiently oblique angle, the later presented object often seems to be perceptibly different in shape – a perceptibly flatter ellipse, for instance.... All this seems to me as plain as it can be, and yet it makes absolutely no difference to the fact that of the surface in question we are *not* prepared to judge that it is perceptibly different from what it was.... It seems, therefore, to be absolutely impossible that the surface seen at the later time should be identical with the object presented then, and the surface seen at the earlier identical with the object presented then, for the simple reason that, whereas with regard to the later seen surface I am not prepared to judge that it is in any way perceptibly different from that seen earlier, it seems that with regard to the later sense-datum I cannot fail to judge that it *is* perceptibly different from the earlier one: the fact that they are perceptibly different simply stares me in the face.
>
> (*SJP*: 243–4)

This argument has a familiar ring. It is in fact just a very clear and sophisticated statement of the argument from illusion. The physical object perceived on two occasions does not change its 'real' shape (or colour, and so on). But *something* must have changed in the interval, for what I am presented with now just is phenomenologically different from what I was presented with then. Therefore, the object I am presented with (i.e., the sense-datum) is not, and cannot be, a part of the surface of the physical object itself. It is an argument which has seemed an absolutely conclusive refutation of direct realism by generations of philosophers. It certainly convinced Descartes, Locke, and Hume. Moore, however, though he considered it a strong argument, did not think that it is quite conclusive. And his reasons for doubt are of fundamental importance, though he later (wrongly, I shall argue) came to reject them as 'nonsensical'.

The whole force of the argument from illusion derives from the claim, which has seemed so very certain to so many philosophers in the Cartesian tradition, that sense-data really do have whatever characteristics they are presented as having. If something in my visual field of presentation appears elliptical, or bent, then something at least really is elliptical (or bent). For I am undeniably presented with what we might call 'an instance of ellipticality'. Thus it seems that the sense-datum, the ultimate subject of the judgement of perception, must really have the property of being elliptical, since the perceived coin is conceded to be round, and the ultimate subject of my judgement cannot be both elliptical and round.

It is this claim, and the reasoning behind it, which Moore calls into question. The claim that there are two different sense-data with different characteristics on the two occasions clearly is a claim with ontological import. Since sense-datum A and sense-'datum B have different characteristics, then A must be a different thing from B. But this claim can be established only if it can be established that sense-datum A really does have characteristic F and sense-datum B really does have characteristic G, where F is a different characteristic from G. If we should attempt to establish a real difference by defining the technical term 'sense-datum' such that sense-data are stipulated to have any and all characteristics they appear to have, then we will have begged the ontological question at issue.

Following the lead of Descartes's use of the term 'idea', most philosophers who have made this basic ontological claim about the nature of sense-data have rested it on phenomenological grounds: the difference in characteristics, and hence in identity, between two sense-data is phenomenologically obvious to anyone who honestly attends to her state of sensory consciousness when she makes a judgement of perception. As Moore himself said, when tempted to make this claim, the perceptible difference between the earlier and the later sense-datum just stares him in the face.

But Moore did not let the matter rest here, as so many other philosophers have done. Instead, he put forward an alternative suggestion for interpreting the phenomenological facts in question:

> What now seems to me possible is that the sense-datum which corresponds to a tree, which I am seeing, when I am a mile off, may not really be perceived to *be* smaller than the one, which corresponds to the same tree, when I see it from a distance of only a hundred yards, but that it is only perceived to *seem* smaller; that the sense-datum which corresponds to the penny, which I am seeing obliquely, is not really perceived to be different in shape from that which corresponded to the penny, when I was straight in front of it, but is only perceived to *seem* different – that all that is perceived is that one *seems* elliptical and the other circular.
>
> (*SJP*: 245)

Moore's terminology is somewhat awkward, but the point he was driving at is by no means nonsensical. In fact, it is of fundamental importance to an understanding of how the Cartesian model of the mind begs the question against direct realism as an analysis of our common-sense realist beliefs about the world we perceive. First let us try to express somewhat more clearly what Moore suggests in this passage; then it can be assessed in relation to the usual claim that sense-data have all (and only) the characteristics they are presented to sensory consciousness as having. To perceive x to be F is to perceive x and to perceive *that it is F*. Thus, if someone perceives x to be F, it follows that x *is* F. Perhaps Moore's intentions regarding the awkward construction ' ... perceive ... to seem ... ' can be explicated as follows: to perceive to seem F is to perceive x, and for x to seem F. Clearly, if someone perceives x to seem F, it does not at all follow that x is F, though it does follow (trivially) that the item x is perceived. It does not follow, however, that the item really has the characteristic F. Support for the view that Moore intended his construction to be understood in this way is the fact that, according to him, all judgements of perception are true, which requires that in a judgement of perception of the form 'That is a circular coin', one truly does perceive the coin and perceives that it is circular. In Moore's words, one perceives it *to be* circular. But this is compatible with that part of its surface which one sees *seeming* elliptical to the perceiver, even though it is not judged to be elliptical. If it *is* the part of the surface with which one is presented, then one is certainly not perceiving it to be elliptical, since it is not elliptical.

It will be recalled that Moore defined 'sense-datum' quasi-

ostensively, as that thing which is the ultimate subject of a judgement of perception: a thing which anyone who knows what to
attend to (or how to attend) will have no difficulty identifying. If
this item *is* part of the surface of the physical object one perceives,
then obviously it cannot actually have some of the characteristics it
is presented as having (i.e., that it seems perceptibly to have) in
cases of the sort under discussion.

Here, then, is the heart of Moore's objection to the argument
from illusion. He argues that we cannot, on phenomenological
grounds alone, settle the question of whether the presented object
(the sense-datum) really has the characteristic *F* or only seems to
have it. For, since the referent of the technical term 'sense-datum'
has been specified ostensively, and without any initial question-
begging ontological commitments or assumptions, it is just not
possible to determine that sense-data do, or that they do not, have
the characteristics they appear to have, without thereby begging
the ontological question.

C. D. Broad (1923) replied to this suggestion of Moore's by
saying that if the presented object is not really *F* then it is difficult
to account for the phenomenological fact that it seems as though
an *F* thing is before one. But this can be met by admitting candidly
that it *is* difficult; indeed, it is impossible to account for this fact on
purely phenomenological grounds. However, it should also be
noted that it is not the proper business of phenomenology to
account for our experiences being as they are, but rather to describe as accurately as possible *how* they are. In any case, the
account traditionally offered of this fact simply presupposes that
the ontology of sensory consciousness recapitulates its ontology.

If we adopt Moore's suggestion, as I think we should, we shall
have to admit that the phenomenology of perceptual consciousness does not force an ontology of perception upon us. In
particular, we cannot conclude, without the aid of non-
phenomenological premises, that whenever it seems to one that
something really elliptical is before one, one is thereby in cognitive
contact with something which really is elliptical. But Moore is
prepared to accept that consequence, for he says that if the view he
is suggesting is true, we shall have to admit

> that the kind of experience which I have expressed by saying
> one *seems* different from the other – '*seems* circular', '*seems*
> blue', '*seems* coloured', and so on – involves an ultimate, not
> further analyzable, kind of psychological relation, not to be
> identified either with that involved in being 'perceived' to be so
> and so, or with that involved in being 'judged' to be so and so;

since a presented object might, in this sense, *seem* to be
elliptical, *seem* to be blue, etc., when it is neither
perceived to be so nor judged to be so.

(*SJP*: 245–6)

If Moore is right, then, no examination of sensory experience or
of its 'contents' is capable of yielding knowledge of the 'real nature'
of what is presented to consciousness. Phenomenology is thus
ontologically barren; or rather, it is ontologically hospitable, since
it does not rule our direct realism, or phenomenalism, or any
other ontological hypothesis which is consistent with sensory experience as carefully and non-prejudicially described.

I think that Moore is right. The phenomenology of sensory
consciousness provides no guarantee that it recapitulates the
ontology of the perceived world. I think that Moore is wrong,
however, in claiming that direct realism, representative realism,
and phenomenalism are merely competing *analyses* of judgements
of perception which have no bearing on the *truth* of our common-
sense beliefs. As will be clear from Chapters 1 and 2, I take
common-sense realism to include as an ingredient a commitment
to the continuous and independent existence of physical objects
that really do have both the so-called primary and secondary
qualities. Any philosophical view which denies this is, I think,
incompatible with common sense; and any philosophical view
which holds that we cannot know whether common-sense realism
is correct or not is also incompatible with common sense. In this, I
think I am in agreement both with defenders of common sense
such as Reid, and also with philosophical critics of common sense
such as Descartes, Locke, and Hume. Moreover, I think that
anyone who believes that phenomenalism is just an analysis of
judgements of perception such as 'This is my hand', and is in no
way incompatible with common sense, is committed to making
such claims as: 'This is my hand, but I don't mean to imply, nor do I
believe, that it exists independently of perception or thought.'
And I think that anyone who believes the same of representative
realism is committed to making such claims as: 'This cherry is red,
but I don't mean to imply, nor do I believe, that it is really red.'
And I am convinced that no one who shares the common-sense
view of the world would accept such a way of construing what is
meant by 'This is a hand' or 'This cherry is red' when these express
judgements of perception. Consequently, I think that Moore is
wrong to claim that the argument from illusion would not threaten
common sense if it were a successful argument.

Moore claimed in 1918 merely to be *inclined* towards the direct-realist analysis of perception. He was not totally confident, subjectively certain, that the argument from illusion would fail. So his claim to be subjectively certain of the truth of the propositions of common sense was misplaced. For in the very paper in which Moore essays to defend common sense, he confesses that he has become convinced that direct realism cannot be true. If, however, one does not believe that direct realism is true, one can hardly be subjectively certain that the common-sense view of the world is true.

Backsliding

By 1925, Moore had abandoned hope for direct realism. He did not actually repudiate the phenomenological argument he used in 1918 to defend a weak version of direct realism against the argument from illusion. But in 'A Defence of Common Sense', after briefly summarizing his 1918 argument, he set forth a new phenomenological argument which convinced him that sense-data could not possibly be identical with parts of the surfaces of physical objects.

> When we see a thing double (have what is called 'a double image' of it), we certainly have *two* sense-data each of which is *of* the surface seen, and which cannot therefore both be identical with it; and yet it seems as if, if any sense-datum is ever identical with the surface *of* which it is a sense-datum, each of these so-called 'images' must be so. It looks, therefore, as if every sense-datum is, after all, only 'representative' of the surface, *of* which it is a sense-datum.
>
> (*DCS*: 56–7)

I do not think that this argument is fatal to direct realism. In fact, I think it rests on basically the same assumption Moore himself discredited in his criticism of the argument from illusion in 1918. If I am right, Moore relapsed into the Cartesian model of the mind between 1918 and 1925: he fell victim to the same pathological reification of our representational mental operations as Descartes, Locke, Berkeley, Hume, and countless adolescents.

When I see double, I have, or sense, two sense-data, according to Moore, each of which is a sense-datum of the same part of the surface of the physical object I am perceiving. Let us call them *A* and *B*. If any sense-datum is identical with the relevant part of the surface of the object, both *A* and *B* are. This seems absurd, of course, because two different things cannot each be identical with one material surface. But it must be remembered that the term 'sense-datum' is being used *merely to denote* that item, whatever it is, which is the ultimate subject of my judgement of perception. Now if this item *is* the relevant part of the surface of the physical object (which, it must be remembered, cannot be determined purely phenomenologically, by examining one's state of consciousness), then the expression 'sense-datum *A*' denotes this part of the surface of the object, and the expression 'sense-datum *B*' also denotes this same part of the surface of the object. The two expressions 'sense-datum *A*' and 'sense-datum *B*' denote the same thing, just as the expressions 'Cicero' and 'Tully' both have the same referent.

Of course, one and the same part of the surface could seem double, could seem to be two items, if one suffers from double vision. But the expression 'sense-datum *A*' cannot, on phenomenological grounds alone, be known to have a different referent from the expression 'sense-datum *B*'. If the technical term 'sense-datum' is introduced by appeal to the phenomenology of sensory consciousness, and is used merely to denote whatever is the ultimate subject of a judgement of perception, then double vision does not constitute an objection to direct realism. So it looks as though Moore was wrong to abandon his 1918 view on the basis of his 'double vision' argument.

The fact that Moore did abandon it, and did so because he thought it was subjectively certain that in double vision he is aware of two distinct things, demonstrates that he was aware of a proposition just as certain on subjective grounds as his certainty of the truth of common-sense propositions. The fact that this proposition is a central element in an argument designed to refute the common-sense view, despite Moore's protestations that it had no such implications, is finally the reason why Moore's principal defence of the common-sense view of the world is not a good argument. The subjective certainty of the propositions of common sense is no guarantee of their truth. We shall have to look elsewhere for a defence of the common-sense view of the world.

The limits of phenomenology

As we have seen, in Moore's examination of the argument from illusion, introspection may be misleading concerning the characteristics of the ultimate subjects of our judgements of perception. If sense-data, as defined by Moore, are ever identical with parts of the surfaces of physical objects, then they may appear to have characteristics that they do not really have, and they may not appear to have characteristics that they really do have. The moral of Moore's argument is that the phenomenology of *perceptual* experience (i.e., the experiences we have when we perceive items and events in our physical environment) underdetermines the ontology of the perceived environment.

We have also seen, in our own examination of Moore's 'double vision' argument, that introspection may be misleading concerning the numerical identity of the ultimate subjects of certain judgements we make, or might be tempted to make, on the basis of the introspectively revealed characteristics of sensory experiences. If Moorean sense-data are ever identical with parts of the surfaces of physical objects, then a particular surface area might, under certain conditions, appear to be (or appear as) two surface areas. The upshot of that examination, then, is that the phenomenology of *sensory* experience (i.e., the experience we have when we *seem* to be perceiving items and events in our physical environment) also underdetermines the ontology of the perceived environment.

What I now wish to argue is the more radical thesis that the phenomenology of sensory experience underdetermines the ontology of sensory experience itself. This is the chief lesson to be learned from the difficulties encountered by Descartes, Locke, Berkeley, Hume, Reid, and Moore. Not only may the ultimate subjects of judgements of perception appear to have characteristics they do not have, and not appear to have characteristics they do have; not only may it seem to me that two perceived items are before me when only one actually is; I may, on the basis of the introspected character of my sensory experience, judge (or be tempted to judge) that I am perceiving some thing in my physical environment when I am not actually sensorily aware of any *entity* at all.

In a totally hallucinatory experience, for instance, I may wrongly judge (or be tempted to judge) that there is some particular physical thing before me in my physical environment. But if sense-data are, by Moore's definition, the ultimate subjects of judgements of perception, I am not in such a case aware of any sense-datum, since the judgement is not a judgement of perception, in Moore's strict sense of that expression. It is not a judgement of perception unless it is true, and based on perceiving whatever it is.

But surely, it will be objected, I have made a judgement, and surely I have made a judgement *about something* which really is present to consciousness. The arguments we considered in the previous section should alert us not to accept this objection too readily. Suppose we alter Moore's definition of 'sense-datum' somewhat, so that the term is said to denote whatever is the ultimate subject of any judgement of the form 'That is a so-and-so', made simply on the basis of one's present sensory experience. Following Moore, this definition is purely phenomenological; it specifies the referent of the term 'sense-datum' by introspective means alone. But then, by the same token, what is here called a sensory experience need not be an experience actually caused by the present stimulation of any of one's sense organs. From a phenomenological point of view, a sensory experience is any experience in which it seems to the conscious subject as though she is perceiving some item or event in her physical environment. Therefore, to avoid begging any crucial ontological questions, we must allow for the possibility that nothing at all, no object, is the ultimate subject of the judgement, other than some feature or aspect of the experience itself. That is, in Reid's words, we may be mistaking an *operation of the mind* for an entity present to the mind. We must allow for the possibility that the referent of the expression 'sense-datum' is not an entity revealed to the conscious subject via the sensory experience.

If it is objected that it is phenomenologically obvious, self-evident, that something, at any rate, is in my 'total field of presentation', and that it is that something, whatever it is, that is the ultimate subject of the judgement, it can be replied that a phenomenological technique for introducing the term 'sense-datum' into the analysis of sensory experience will not bear this ontological weight. To insist, on phenomenological grounds alone, that there is some actual thing or entity which is being judged to be so-and-so is to beg the central question at issue in the analysis.

If the temptation to beg the central ontological question is resisted, what alternative is there for the analysis of judgements of perception, and for the analysis of sensory experiences generally? One alternative is Reid's proposal that sensations are 'operations of the mind' which play a causal role in perception, not objects before consciousness which play an evidential role. Another alternative is the 'adverbial' analysis of such experiences recommended by Roderick Chisholm (1957). According to this analysis, which resembles Reid's view purged of the doctrine that sensations function as signs, when we undergo a sensory experience, that is, an experience in which it seems as though there is some object with certain characteristics before us, we are experiencing in a certain *way*, but there is not necessarily always some item or object (except in the grammatical sense) that we are thus experiencing. Phenomenological description, then, is to be construed as the description of the *manner* in which one is experiencing, in which

151

one is mentally representing: it is the way the experience seems to the experiencer, rather than as a description of what (in the sense of what item or thing) one is experiencing.

Of course, it generally seems to the experiencing subject as though some item is being experienced. And in normal cases of perception, the way one is experiencing is the causal product of some item in one's environment being the way it is. If we supplement the adverbial analysis of sensory experience with a causal analysis of perception, we can say that perceiving some physical object to be so-and-so is nothing other than having an experience of its seeming as though there is a so-and-so item in one's environment, which experience is the causal consequence of that item's really being in one's environment and really being so-and-so.

However, it can also happen that one experiences in the same way that one would be experiencing if one were perceiving a so-and-so item in one's physical environment, but the experience is not the normal causal consequence of a so-and-so item being in one's environment. In fact, in hallucinatory cases, there is no item of that sort there to be the cause of the experience. In such a case, it seems to one that one is perceiving a physical thing, but, though one is experiencing in that *way*, there is no *thing* that one is thereby experiencing. One is having an experience of a certain sort with different causal antecedents from the causal antecedents in genuine normal perception.

If this analysis of perception, and of sensory experience generally, is on the right track, then we can see why the phenomenology of perception underdetermines its ontology. Although Moore always believed that sense-data were actual things that we experience, his defence of direct realism against the argument from illusion, based as it was on an insistence that we do not try to get more out of the phenomenology of perceptual experience than is genuinely there, paved the way for an analysis of those propositions of common sense called judgements of perception, which is continuous with the analysis of all 'experiential' propositions.

It is also, of course, an analysis that no longer really has any need for a term that functions in the way that 'sense-datum' functions in the philosophy of G. E. Moore, or 'idea' in the philosophies of the theorists of ideas. Sometimes, when we make a judgement of the form 'That is a so-and-so', based solely upon our present sensory experience, there is some item, a physical object, which is the ultimate subject of the judgement. But sometimes, as in hallucination, there is no such item. The sense-datum analysis, pioneered by Moore but essentially a variant of the Cartesian model of the mind, rests on the avoidable, and deleterious, presupposition, never fully examined by Descartes, Locke, Berkeley, Hume, or by most of the sense-datum philosophers of the twentieth century, that there is always some entity which is the ultimate subject of all judgements of this sort, simply because it phenomenologically seems as though there is.

Part four
The Defence of Common Sense

8

A defence of common sense

It might be helpful to pause for a moment and take stock of the argument so far. I have argued: (a) that the common-sense view of the world is a shared network of beliefs about the world and our relation to it, which is expressed in virtually all of our thought and behaviour; (b) that rational psychology and common-sense realism are the two major constituents of the common-sense view; (c) that we make use of rational psychology and common-sense realism in defending our claims about the way the world is and in explaining our own and others' behaviour, for which reason the common-sense view of the world deserves to be thought of as an explanatory 'theorette'; (d) that four cognitive abilities are essential to the common-sense view: the ability to engage in meta-representation, (which is itself a prerequisite for) the ability to make an appearance–reality distinction, the ability to recognize representational diversity, and the ability to recognize representational change; (e) that none of these abilities is present in us before about 18 months, and the latter three do not appear until about age 4; from which it follows that until we are 4 or so we do not fully share the common-sense view of the world; (f) that a representational model of the mind is embedded in the latter three cognitive abilities, and its development at about age 4 accounts for the virtually simultaneous acquisition of these abilities at that period.

I have provided a summary at this point in order to highlight the fact that I have not so far attempted to defend, or even to assess, the common-sense view, though I have examined in some detail, in Chapters 6 and 7, the arguments of the two most notable defenders of common sense: Thomas Reid and G. E. Moore. In this concluding chapter my aim is to outline a defence of the common-sense view of the world, drawing heavily on the developmental data surveyed in Chapters 3 and 4, and on the analysis of the cognitive abilities underlying common sense presented in Chapter 2.

Common sense and successful action

To the extent that their speech and other behaviour enables us to attribute an implicit view about the world and our relation to it to children 3 years of age and younger, it is not just different from the view implicitly held by everyone over the age of about 4, it is defective in certain salient ways. These young children have systematically false beliefs about their own and other peoples' representational states, and these false beliefs tend to lead them to engage in behaviour which is systematically inappropriate to the way the world is, with the not infrequent result that their behavioural goals are frustrated. Let me explain in some detail what I am claiming.

If I think that my tennis racket is at this moment hanging on a peg in the basement, then I am in a particular first-order representational state *vis-à-vis* my tennis racket, which state is also instantiated in anyone else who at this moment believes that my tennis racket is hanging on a peg in the basement. Suppose that I think that my tennis racket is hanging on a peg in the basement because I am actually in the basement looking at it. At the metarepresentational level, if anyone else is in the basement with me, sees the racket and so comes to believe that it is hanging there, then we probably each believe that the other believes that the tennis racket is hanging there on the peg, since each of us is probably aware that the other is in the basement and looking at the racket. So in general, if I think that someone else perceives F when I perceive F, but they don't in fact perceive F, then I have a false belief about their representational state. Similarly, if I think that someone else believes what I believe, and they don't, or that someone else is aware of what I want, and they aren't, then I have false beliefs about their representational states. If I then predict (or anticipate) that they will perform some action A, based on my false belief about their representational state, my prediction is likely to be falsified by what they in fact do. Likewise, if I myself undertake a course of action based in some important measure on a false belief about their representational state, my action aim is likely to be frustrated, in that I am likely not to accomplish what I intended to.

For example, suppose it is important that we meet, and I leave you a note saying that I will meet you tonight at 8 o'clock at Melissa's, assuming that you know who Melissa is and where she lives. If you don't know one of these things, then the chances are that I will be cooling my heels at Melissa's without meeting you there. The same will happen if I falsely assume that you will read

158

the note before 8 tonight, or falsely assume that you are free to meet me at 8 tonight. In general, successful action (that is, roughly, action in which one accomplishes what one set out to accomplish), depends fairly heavily on having true beliefs about the world. Successful co-operative action depends fairly heavily on my having true beliefs about what the other co-operating persons believe and want, and on them having true beliefs about what I believe and want. Occasionally one may strike it lucky, and accomplish one's goals despite one's false beliefs. But it strains credulity to suppose that there is no systematic relation between true beliefs (about the world, and about other people's representational states) and successful action.

Since the evidence surveyed in Chapter 3 suggests that very young children before about 18 months of age are incapable of forming second-order mental representations, it would be misleading to describe them as having *false* beliefs about people's representational states. It would be less tendentious to describe them as lacking certain important *true* beliefs about people's representational states. The fact is that they don't yet use the mentalistic vocabulary. Since they don't verbally ascribe mental states to themselves and others, we lack the grounds in their case that we have in attributing second-order mental representations to other language-using adults. Yet, as we have seen in Chapter 3, long before the age of 18 months, children are capable of shared attention and reference; they have developed some primitive awareness of the difference between passive objects and animate agents; they can engage in rudimentary social co-operation, as in the use of a toy as a topic for shared play; they are capable of forming plans; and they use gestures, and then words, to request co-operation from others. But infants are also frequently frustrated in getting the world to answer to their desires, as any harried parent knows. And frequently their frustration stems from their ignorance of the relevant representational states of others. Instead of describing them as acting on the false belief that someone else knows what they want or sees what they see, perhaps it is better to describe them as acting in ignorance of the fact that the other does not know what they want or cannot see what they see. In any case, they frequently act in such a way that we have reason to believe that their behavioural aims are frustrated, but the actions would have been successful if they had possessed certain beliefs about others' representational states.

Thus we who are attempting to explain their behaviour can interpret them as acting rationally, albeit unsuccessfully, if we construe them as acting out of a representational deficit. Either they lack a crucial belief about the world, or they lack a crucial metarepresentational belief. Our motivation for adopting the intentional stance towards human infants (see Dennett 1978) is similar to our motivation in adopting it toward infrahuman species. We can interpret, explain, and systematically anticipate their behaviour if we adopt the intentional stance towards them, whereas their behaviour is unintelligible to us if we do not do so. The interpretative and explanatory gain justifies the use of the interpretative and explanatory framework.

The situation is somewhat different in the case of children in the 2–3-year-old range. We have good reason to think that they have acquired the ability to form second-order mental representations, for they can engage in behaviour, such as pretence, and can make appropriate comments on the success or failure of their own plans, which behaviour would be unintelligible without the supposition that they can represent and reason about other people's representational states; and they have acquired some proficiency in the appropriate use of the mentalistic vocabulary in conversation. But we have also seen, in Chapter 3, experimental evidence that they have not yet acquired the three cognitive abilities that depend on subscribing to a representational model of the mind's functioning. The child who says that the red-cellophane-covered green cat both looks black and really and truly is black, who says that the sponge-rock both is a sponge and looks like one, doesn't recognize that we mentally represent things when we perceive them, and that the way they are mentally represented in perception may sometimes differ from their 'true' nature. The child who predicts that her friend who hasn't seen what's inside the Smartie box will think that the box contains pencils doesn't yet understand that someone else can represent the same situation differently from oneself. When she gives every indication of being surprised to see pencils emerging from the Smartie box, but then says that she believed that the box contained pencils even before it was opened, she shows that she has difficulty recognizing that just a few moments ago she represented a situation differently from the way she now knows it to be.

These are representational deficits that show up in behaviour. Three-year-olds are unsuccessful in these tasks. Presumably they want to give the right answer to the experimenter's questions, but they cannot, because of their representational deficit. Their systematic use of the mentalistic vocabulary shows that they do attribute representational states to others. They don't use the terms 'belief' and 'desire' at this age, but they say things such as 'She thinks...', or 'He knows...', or 'She wants...', or 'He is trying to...'; and they say these things in contexts where they are obviously trying to make a sincere contrast between the way the world is and someone else's beliefs, in order to explain what they or someone else has done or to predict what someone will do.

The representational deficits of the 3-year-olds show up not only in their behaviour on experimental tasks, but in their everyday behaviour outside the laboratory as well. It is particularly evident in their inability to play deceptive games such as hide-and-seek effectively, where one must be able to adopt the perceptual perspective of the one who is 'it'. They are also unable to engage effectively in strategic games, which rely on the ability to hypothesize what another person is likely to believe about a situation, or about one's own beliefs, and to make use of that hypothesis competitively in one's own reasoning. Facility at these social games does not begin to emerge until after 4 years of age, as we have seen.

Now we have no less reason to attribute rationality to 3-year-olds than to their infant brothers and sisters. In situations not requiring these particular cognitive abilities they are intelligible enough as rational agents. So it seems justified to describe them, in the types of situation we have been surveying, as acting on inadequate beliefs, which beliefs are a function of their representational deficit. And these actions tend to be systematically unsuccessful, in that the failure of the act can be attributed to their ignorance of representational diversity, or representational change, or the appearance–reality distinction. Once one is aware of the representational deficits in children, one can also successfully predict the situations in which their actions will be successful.

Coming to share the common-sense view of the world makes a difference in one's life. Five-year-olds and adults have a hard enough time accomplishing the goals they set for themselves; but their failures can very seldom be attributed to false beliefs arising from the representational deficits characteristic of very young children. That is, infants and very young children tend to be systematically unsuccessful in their actions in the same type of situations in which older children and adults tend to be systematically successful: situations in which the difference between success and frustration depends on one's ability to recognize representational diversity and representational change, or to make 'adult' appearance–reality distinctions.

Of course, to talk about success and frustration in this context makes sense only if it makes sense to attribute some of the same desires, intentions, and plans to these very young children that we attribute to our fellow adults, such as the desire to remain hidden from the sight of the other participants in hide-and-seek, or the intention to give correct answers to questions about what others will think is in the Smarties box. In other words, we have to interpret their behaviour, including their utterances, against a background of other beliefs and intentions that we think they share with us. As a condition of their behaviour being intelligible to us as rational (albeit unsuccessful) action at all, we must adopt the principle of charity: we must attribute to them as many of our own ordinary beliefs and desires as we can to provide this background of interpretation. It is only against a background of shared beliefs and desires that we can recognize those ways in which our beliefs and intentions differ from theirs, and thus have any hope of explaining and predicting their actions. It is only against such a background that cognitive psychologists can devise experiments to test hypotheses about the cognitive capacities of children, or even of adults, for that matter.

What we recognize, as a consequence of our efforts to interpret the behaviour of these very young children, is that there is a systematic, law-like difference between our behaviour and theirs in precisely those contexts in which successful action requires the specific metarepresentational ability to make an appearance–reality distinction, the ability to recognize representational change, or the ability to recognize representational diversity. And these abilities are manifested, in particular situations, in the having of certain beliefs that someone who lacks these abilities does not have in the same circumstances. Usually, when we ask ourselves why someone is doing whatever he is observed to be doing, we assume that his beliefs are appropriate to the situation, that is, that he has the same information about the way the relevant bit of the world is as we have. We assume that people are cognizant of the gross features of their immediate environment, just as we are. The focus of our enquiry is usually the person's desiderative state: what does he *want*, such that *this* observed behaviour can be interpreted as a rational action? We think that the beliefs relevant to the situation are more likely to be shared, since we believe that they are caused in us by our cognitive contact with objective, mind-independent features of the environment. But people's desiderative states, what they want the world to be like, are less likely to be shared. Being similarly situated in the same environment is likely to produce in two people similar beliefs about what is the case. But it is much less likely to produce in them the same desiderative state, owing to differences in emotional state, long-term goals, personal history, and so on.

So in those cases in which a person's observed behaviour gives us no reason to suppose that his beliefs about his environment are different from our own, we hold his epistemic state constant, and hypothesize as to his desiderative state. In those situations in which a person's desiderative state is salient to us, however, and the person nevertheless acts in a puzzling or inappropriate way, we need to adopt the opposite strategy in order to render his behaviour intelligible to us as rational action. In these cases, we hold desiderative state constant and hypothesize as to epistemic state.

If we attribute to the 3-year-olds the same desiderative states that we would attribute to ourselves in the same circumstances – if, that is, we hold desiderative state constant – then the difference that will explain their systematic tendency to unsuccessful action in these circumstances is a difference in belief. But the difference between what we believe in these contexts and what they believe is very revealing. To be precise, we succeed and they fail because we have relevant beliefs constitutive of the common-sense view of the world and the 3-year-olds do not, and also because differences in belief lead to differences in action if relevant desiderative states are the same. The law-like difference in behaviour is thus explained by the fact that we are fully-fledged rational psychologists and common-sense realists, whereas the young children are not.

The same type of argument supports both common-sense realism and rational psychology, as can be shown by two examples. Suppose Melissa has an inordinate appetite for wild cherries. The only small, black, smooth-skinned berries she has ever seen are wild cherries. Now red baneberries look very much like wild cherries, except that they are red, not black. Red baneberries are also poisonous. So it is indeed fortunate that they differ in colour; otherwise wild-cherry addicts offered a bowl of baneberries might make an unpleasant mistake. Melissa's mother has frequently warned her against eating red baneberries, and has told her how to tell them apart. If a malicious cognitive developmentalist were to show 3-year-old Melissa some red baneberries on a green plate, then in her presence place a green transparent film over the plate and ask her whether she wanted to eat some of the berries, she might well say yes, since she thinks these berries really and truly are black. After all, they look black. You and I, gentle reader, would make no such mistake, since we believe that they look black, but are really and truly red.

Suppose that Melissa and Jason see the ice-cream vendor at the park entrance and Melissa asks Jason to buy her a cone. Jason has to go somewhere on an errand, but he agrees to return in an hour's time and buy her a cone. (Jason shouldn't leave his 3-year-old

163

sister alone for an hour, of course; but we won't tell on him.) After Jason has gone, the ice-cream vendor tells Melissa that he is going to move his van to the other entrance to the park, hidden from the first entrance by a grove of trees. Melissa follows the ice-cream vendor to the other park entrance and waits patiently, but vainly, for Jason to appear. She does not realize that Jason will go where he thinks the ice-cream vendor is. She thinks he will go where the ice-cream vendor actually is. She does not realize that people's actions are a function of their desires and their beliefs.

By applying the same criterion of successful action uniformly both to ourselves and to children 3 years old and younger (the criterion of accomplishing what one sets out to accomplish, which, after all, is the only criterion of successful action we know how to apply to them), our actions in certain circumstances are seen to be systematically successful, and theirs are not, because we have certain true beliefs that they do not have. But since these beliefs are precisely those which are embedded in the common-sense view of the world, and since what differentiates us from them in the relevant respect is that we share the common-sense view and they do not, I am inclined to conclude that the common-sense view of the world is correct. But perhaps it would be more judicious to conclude merely that the common-sense view is highly confirmed by the differential and systematic success of adults as compared to children in these crucial circumstances.

An anticipated objection considered

I anticipate an objection from the detractors of 'folk psychology' and 'folk metaphysics', to the effect that my defence of common sense begs the question at issue at the outset merely by *describing* some adult behaviour as 'successful action' and contrasting it with certain children's behaviour, which is described as 'unsuccessful action'. For it is constitutive of the 'common-sense myth' (as the detractors would characterize it) that an action is a piece of behaviour caused by epistemic state and desiderative state, and the criterion of 'successful action' that has been used in this defence is 'action in which the desiderative state that was one of its causes was satisfied as a result of the action', thus compounding the question-begging definition of 'action'.

I think this objection misses the point. The vocabulary of action, belief, desire, and so on, is an integral part of a 'theorette-ical' framework of description and explanation we and our ancestors have devised in order to make our own and others' behaviour intelligible. From within that framework we have criteria for identifying some behaviour as the performance of an action and some as 'mere' behaviour. These criteria enjoin us to deploy the 'theorette-ical' vocabulary by attributing specific epistemic states and specific desiderative states to people, and to differentially predict their behaviour on the basis of these attributions. It also requires us to account for their behaviour retroactively, and to 'predict' counterfactually what they would do or would have done, by the deployment of the same theorette-ical framework. This framework also provides criteria for identifying some actions as successful, others as unsuccessful, which are independent of the criteria used to identify behaviour as an action (whether successful or not). When we have good reason to attribute a particular desiderative state to a person, we count his action successful if the desiderative state is satisfied by the outcome of the action, unsuccessful if it is not.

It is true that we couldn't even *describe* our behaviour as the performance of actions, much less explain it, if we didn't use the vocabulary and categories of common sense that are embedded in natural languages.[1] But the explanatory use of the vocabulary and categories embedded in natural languages is not intellectually illegitimate. It is the systematic employment of a theorette supporting systematic predictions, which are confirmed by observed behaviour again and again. In each individual case in which it is confirmed it is weakly confirmed, to be sure. The theorette underdetermines the data; other theorettes (or full-blown theories, for that matter) might well be confirmed by the same data in that individual case. But the massive number and variety of cases in which the theorette receives weak confirmation adds enormous cumulative support to the theorette.[2] When we find a crucial systematic difference between the beliefs of adults who (as a group) tend to act successfully in a certain category of circumstances and those of children who (as a group) tend to act unsuccessfully in the same category of circumstances, that provides cumulative empirical support also for the theorette of which the adult beliefs are the hypothesized expressions.

There's nothing question-begging in any of this. Chapter 1 established that we are rational psychologists and common-sense realists. Chapter 2 established that the beliefs required for rational psychology and common-sense realism require of the believer the ability to make certain metacognitive distinctions. Chapter 3 established that young children don't have these abilities, hence don't have these beliefs. But these same young children often engage in actions which can succeed as rational action only if they have these beliefs and the beliefs are true. We adults have these beliefs, and we tend to succeed when we engage in these sorts of actions. The best explanation of this is that the beliefs we have are true. What are these beliefs? They are the beliefs embedded in rational psychology and common-sense realism, beliefs about the cognitive relationship between mind and the world and about why people act as they do.

Reid and Moore again

How does the defence of common sense presented in this chapter compare with the arguments in defence of common sense advanced by Reid and by Moore? Although Reid listed propositions which can reasonably be considered elements of rational psychology among his 'first principles of contingent truths', the four arguments he offered in defence of common sense seem designed specifically to defend common-sense realism. The first argument I examined in Chapter 6, to the effect that since common sense is true, no sound argument can lead to a conclusion contradicting any proposition of common sense. Thus, any argument that does have a conclusion contradicting common sense must rest on at least one false premiss or on an error in reasoning.

On the face of it, this argument is flagrantly question-begging. But if it is interpreted in the spirit of one of Moore's arguments, which it closely resembles, then it claims merely that the propositions of common sense are subjectively certain, and asserts that any argument contrary to common sense will at some point rest on a premiss which is less certain than the common-sense proposition it impugns, or on some error of reasoning. Reid did go on to argue that the sceptical arguments against common-sense realism on the part of adherents of the Cartesian model of the mind arise from specific errors inherent in that conception of the mind. Reid's third defence of common sense is related to this criticism. But even if his arguments do dispose of Cartesian-inspired scepticism concerning common sense, there may be other arguments against common-sense realism not examined by Reid, which rest on subjectively certain premisses and contain no errors of reasoning. In the absence of any positive argument for the correctness of common sense, such as the one advanced in the present chapter, Reid's bald claim that no sound argument can contradict a fundamental principle of common sense is just a hollow boast, perhaps engendered by misplaced subjective certainty.

Moore's version of this argument is flawed by his mistaken insistence that a commitment to direct realism is not a component of common sense but is only one of many candidates for the analysis of common-sense judgements of perception. Although he presented a very strong argument in defence of direct realism against the fundamental premiss of the argument from illusion, his eventual abandonment of that argument on the grounds that it is incompatible with something of which he was subjectively certain – namely, that the sense-data he directly apprehends cannot be identical with part of the surface of the physical object he perceives – puts paid to his claim that any argument against the common-sense view will rest at some point on an error in reasoning or on a premiss less than subjectively certain. The argument from illusion, in the version Moore examined, contains no logical errors, and rests squarely on the phenomenological claim about the ontological nature of sense-data which Moore thought he knew with certainty to be true.

Moore's other arguments, that anyone who claims that no common-sense propositions are true is guilty of self-refutation, and that anyone who claims that we cannot know that any common-sense propositions are true is guilty of self-contradiction, are extremely feeble, as we saw in Chapter 7. So, I argued in Chapter 6, is Reid's argument that since the perceptually grounded beliefs of common sense are, like the faculty of reason, products of 'the mint of Nature', reason has no greater claim to be the arbiter of truth than sense perception.

I argued that Reid's fourth line of defence, to the effect that even theoretical sceptics are practical adherents to the common-sense view, is an *ad hominem* argument, even though the claim it contains is true. If, however, Reid were to focus on our practical success, which results from our common-sense beliefs, and if he were to argue that the practical success is best explained by the hypothesis that these beliefs, which nature constrains even the sceptic to have, are actually true, then he would be advancing an argument similar to the one advanced in this chapter. But it is doubtful that Reid actually intended his 'even the sceptic can't help believing these things' argument to be interpreted in this way. And even if he did intend it to be understood as an inference to the best explanation, he did not, as my argument does, show which specific components of the common-sense view account for the success of specific actions in specific situations.

Davidson's defence of common sense

The theory of interpretation that Donald Davidson has been developing for many years has implications similar in many respects to the defence of common sense that I have presented in this

chapter (see Davidson 1984a). He draws some of those implications himself in a recent paper (1984b), though he does not therein
explicitly represent himself as defending the common-sense view.
The theoretical problem of interpretation applies as much to the
task of interpreting the utterances of someone one thinks speaks
one's own language as it does to that of interpreting the initially
unintelligible utterances of the neighbouring French, the exotic
Yuktalvians, the alien Alpha Centaurians, or the ancient Mayans;
for the sounds one hears (or the marks one sees) are utterances in
one's own language only if the speaker meant by them what one
interprets them as meaning.

To interpret individual utterances is to assign them a meaning in
a particular language: it is to interpret a particular utterance *s* of
theirs as meaning (in English) that so-and-so, which according to
Davidson is captured by setting forth the truth conditions (in
English) of what we construe to be a sentence *s* in their language.
For example, we might interpret Nicole's utterance of 'Il pleut' as
meaning (as said by Nicole on that occasion) that it is raining (in
Nicole's vicinity at the time of utterance), because we take 'Il pleut'
to be a sentence of French that is true (when asserted by a speaker
of French) if and only if it is raining (in the vicinity of the speaker,
and so on). To say that the speaker asserts a sentence is to say that
she publicly represents herself as holding it to be true. Having
constructed a theory of interpretation for Nicole (namely, that she
is a French speaker who is speaking French now), we can test the
theory empirically by observing whether she (nearly always)
asserts, or assents to what we have interpreted as French sentences
when their truth conditions are satisfied.

According to Davidson, in order to interpret the utterances of
others as meaningful speech, it is necessary to construe those
utterances as expressing their beliefs and intentions. In particular,
we must construe some of their utterances as assertoric sentences
expressing what they hold to be true. But we might be convinced
that a person has asserted something, and even be convinced that
she has meant what she said (i.e., that she has said it because she
holds it to be true), and yet we might not have the remotest clue as
to what her words meant. To get the interpretative enterprise off
the ground, to get a purchase on what speakers mean by their
utterances, Davidson argues that we must not only assume that
they say what they believe, but that most of what they believe
actually is true by our own lights. That is, we must extend to them
the principle of charity and assume that we share with them a vast
network of mainly true beliefs about the world. This is not to say
that we must find everything they believe true or even plausible.

168

We may interpret some of their utterances as expressing mistaken beliefs. We may find some of their beliefs very exotic, even absurd (by our lights). But unless we assume that we share with them such mundane beliefs as that it is raining (when we are standing with them in a downpour), then we are not even going to be able to construe them as rational creatures whose emitted noises are meaningful utterances. It is only against the background of this assumed agreement that whatever disagreements there are can be discerned. It is only against this background that the utterances of a speaker could ever be seen to confirm or disconfirm a theory of interpretation. Thus, the assumption of a vast, and well-grounded, agreement in beliefs is a precondition of the possibility of interpretation.

The assumption of a shared network of largely true beliefs is not merely a precondition of interpretation, according to Davidson. It is justified by the success of the interpretative enterprise. We have good reason to believe that the interpretative enterprise does succeed. Remember that we not only need to interpret those whose utterances we initially find unintelligible, we also interpret those whom we hypothesize to be speaking our own language: we interpret them as meaning by 'It's raining' what we mean by it. Our success in interpreting one another, though, gives us good reason to believe that we share with others a vast network of mutually coherent beliefs about the world and about one another. But our network of beliefs would not be coherent, and we would not be mutually interpretable, unless most of our beliefs were caused in us by states of affairs independently obtaining in the world. Hence the coherence of our beliefs with one another is an index of their truth. In Davidson's view, this amounts to having justification for saying that we have a vast amount of knowledge about the world.

Although Davidson can be interpreted as having constructed an elegant general defence of our common-sense beliefs, he does not attempt a taxonomy, a categorization of the basic component elements of the common-sense view. He argues that we have good reason to claim to know that most of our beliefs are true; but he does not identify any particular belief, or any particular type of belief, which we know to be true. It is a virtue of my own defence of the common-sense view that I base it on an explicit account of the basic constituents of common sense, and of the underlying cognitive capacities required of anyone who shares the common-sense view. This account thus shows the link between certain of our *epistemic powers* and an *epistemological justification* of the fundamental tenets of common-sense realism, which are implicated in the specific beliefs Davidson would have us attribute to those we wish to interpret. The differential performance of 3-year-olds and adults in situations in which the basic abilities underlying common sense are at issue, I have argued, gives us good reason to claim that certain specific beliefs are true: namely, those that underwrite the successful performance.

Furthermore, what I am construing as Davidson's defence of common sense relies on our ability to posit, and to confirm empirically, shared belief structures among mutually interpretable beings. His argument may be paraphrased as follows: since my beliefs are mainly true, and since I can interpret someone by attributing to her the tendency to believe a sentence *s* when and only when *s* is true, and since my interpretation theory is empirically confirmed, I have good reason to believe that both of us have mainly true beliefs.

However, I have used the developmental data to argue that the truth of the beliefs we interpret other adults as sharing with us is vouchsafed by the salient *differences* in belief structures between adults and very young children. It is because we cannot interpret them as believing what we believe, and also because those very beliefs lead to successful actions on our part, but their absence leads to unsuccessful beliefs on the children's part, that we have good reason to hold that these very beliefs, and not merely a vague 'most of our beliefs', are true. Hence we have good reason to claim that the common-sense view of the world is true.

Attributing beliefs to languageless creatures

There is another, deeper difference between Davidson's view and my own. Davidson has argued (1975, 1982) that in order to be capable of belief, one must have the concept of belief.

> We have the idea of belief only from the role of belief in the interpretation of language, for as a private attitude it is not intelligible except as an adjustment to the public norm provided by language. It follows that a creature must be a member of a speech community if it is to have the concept of belief. And given the dependence of other attitudes on belief, we can say more generally that only a creature that can interpret speech can have the concept of a thought.
>
> Can a creature have a belief if it does not have the concept of belief? It seems to me that it cannot, and for this reason. Someone cannot have a belief unless he understands the possibility of being mistaken, and this requires grasping the contrast between truth and error – true belief and false belief.

> But this contrast, I have argued, can emerge only in the context
> of interpretation, which alone forces us to the idea of an
> objective, public truth.
>
> (Davidson 1975: 170)

Oddly enough, he admits (1982) that we can often successfully
explain and predict the behaviour of prelinguistic children and
animals by attributing beliefs to them, and that we have no hope of
making sense of their behaviour unless we attribute beliefs and
other attitudes to them. And he admits that this may well constitute a practical justification for attributing beliefs to them. But he
insists that we nevertheless have reason to deny that they really
have beliefs, since we have reason to doubt that they possess the
concept of objective truth, and hence cannot possess the concept
of belief.

Davidson's theory of interpretation is essentially a theory of
linguistic interpretation, whereas what I have been arguing is that
common sense is (in part) a theorette of interpretation of our
behaviour in general, not just linguistic behaviour. Davidson
wants to give a theoretical account of how we can specify the
meaning of someone's linguistic utterances. I want to provide an
account (more informal than Davidson's, to be sure) of our ability
to find the behaviour of people and animals intelligible.

Now my view is in accord with Davidson's in attributing certain
beliefs to people 4 years old and older who give evidence of having
the cognitive abilities outlined in Chapter 2. It seems reasonable to
attribute to them the concept of belief, because they use words
appropriately that play the epistemic role 'belief' plays, even
though they may not use the word 'belief' when attributing beliefs
to others or to themselves. (They will typically say 'I thought...' or
'She thinks...'.) The contextually appropriate use of these expressions depends, as does 'belief', on having the concept of objective
truth; and it depends on grasping the contrast between truth and
error. It is likely that Davidson would allow that younger children,
who show evidence of metarepresentation, but not the more
sophisticated abilities depending on metarepresentation, have a
concept of belief, for they too seem to interpret one another and
adults by means of expressions such as 'He thinks...'. However, I
have said that a feature of common sense is our attribution of
beliefs to prelinguistic infants, and even to members of some
infrahuman species, and Davidson holds that common sense is in
error on this front, theoretically, if not practically.

Now I agree with Davidson that the concept of belief is
essentially bound up with the concept of truth. Therefore I agree
with him that one cannot have the concept of belief without having

the concept of truth. I also agree that to have the concept of truth requires grasping the contrast between truth and error, and hence being able to attribute belief to someone requires understanding the possibility of being mistaken. But it does not follow from this that one cannot believe something without having the concept of belief. It doesn't even follow that one cannot be in a state best described as holding some sentence true, which is Davidson's favoured characterization of belief. Being able to *attribute* beliefs, I would urge, is different from being able to have them. Believing essentially involves the possibility of error; but it does not follow that it involves understanding that possibility. In the terminology of Chapter 2, believing is a first-order representational state. Having beliefs about beliefs, including attributing beliefs to oneself and others, is a second-order or metarepresentational state.

We might usefully think of belief (as opposed to metabelief: belief about belief) on the analogy of a bet (see de Sousa 1971). Believing that the berries are wild cherries is a representational state that differs from the representational state of merely imagining, or entertaining the thought, that the berries are wild cherries. In both cases one represents berries as wild cherries. But in the case of belief, one is disposed to act in a certain way, as it were to bet on the truth of the sentence 'Those berries are wild cherries' by acting in a certain way (for example, eating the berries, if one loves wild cherries and thinks these are wild cherries). Acting on a belief, then, can be likened to actually placing one's bet. The pay-off, if one is right, if one's belief is true, is the success of whatever action is contingent on the truth of the sentence. (Of course, it will also be contingent on other factors, such as one's motor control.) The penalty for error is typically the frustration of the goal for the sake of which the action was taken.

Thus we are justified in attributing beliefs to infants and infrahumans to the extent that it permits us to account for their behaviour as intentional actions, the success of which is contingent upon the truth of the sentence(s) we use in describing the beliefs we attribute to them.

But how can we presume to attribute beliefs of determinate content to languageless creatures? Davidson is very doubtful that the attribution of any specific belief is ever uniquely justified by the circumstances.

The intensionality we make so much of in the attribution of thoughts is very hard to make much of when speech is not present. The dog, we say, knows that its master is home. But does it know that Mr. Smith (who is his master), or that the president of the bank (who is that same master) is home? We have no real idea how to settle, or make sense of, these questions....

These considerations will probably be less persuasive to dog lovers than to others, but in any case they do not constitute an argument. At best what we have shown, or claimed, is that unless there is behaviour that can be interpreted as speech, the evidence will not be adequate to justify the fine distinctions we are used to making in the attribution of thoughts. If we persist in attributing desires, beliefs or other attitudes under these conditions, our attributions and consequent explanations of actions will be seriously underdetermined in that many alternative systems of attribution, many alternative explanations, will be equally justified by the available data.

(Davidson 1975: 163–4)

I tend to agree with the last two sentences of this passage, but I am not for that reason inclined to wring my hands in despair at the prospect of usefully explaining and predicting the behaviour of infants and infrahumans by means of the attribution of beliefs and other attitudes. First of all, the question at issue is not the nature of belief, but the justification of using particular sentences to characterize the beliefs we attribute. Since infants and infrahumans are bereft of language, it is conceded by all parties that their beliefs cannot really amount to holding certain English sentences true. The choice of an appropriate English sentence to characterize the belief, though, is part of the task of making coherent sense of a whole pattern of behaviour, and is essentially related to the decision of how to characterize the action that we are led to attribute on the basis of the behaviour in the circumstances.

Suppose we see a dog chasing a squirrel. The squirrel runs up a nearby beech tree. From our vantage point, we see the squirrel then jump from the beech to a branch of a nearby oak. The dog, meanwhile, is standing at the base of the beech, furiously barking up the wrong tree. I want to say that the dog is behaving in the observed way in part because of what it believes, and that in this case it is acting on a false belief. What belief?

The sentence I choose to characterize the belief I attribute to the dog will be one that is designed to make the behaviour intelligible as (sort of) rational action on the part of the dog. But if I am giving a verbal explanation to someone else, I might add a bit of extra information, relying on what I think my audience will understand, to make what I say optimally informative to my audience. So I might say that the dog believes that the squirrel is in the beech tree. If I am aware that the squirrel is Ralph, and think that my audience knows that there is a squirrel called Ralph much on my mind lately, I may even say that the dog believes that Ralph is in the beech tree. If I think my audience is aware that the beech tree in question is called 'the charter beech' by the local folk, I may say that the dog believes that Ralph is in the charter beech. But of course I do not seriously think that the dog identifies the squirrel as the one called Ralph, nor even that the dog thinks of the creature up the tree as a squirrel. For all I know, the dog might have acted in the same way had it been a mongoose. Nor do I attribute dendrological knowledge to the dog. Had the tree been a chestnut, or a telephone pole, the dog might well be behaving in the same way. The finer distinctions we sometimes make in attributing beliefs to infants and animals play a useful and informative conversational role, but they frequently do not play a serious explanatory role.

On the other hand, a characterization that is too coarse will not play any explanatory role at all. It will not enable us to make the dog's behaviour intelligible as an action. 'The dog believes that something is somewhere' doesn't have any bite at all in helping us make sense of the dog's frantic barking at the base of that particular tree. I don't, after all, think that the dog is behaving as it is because it is periodically seized by the uncontrollable urge to bark at the base of trees.

I want to connect the dog's current behaviour with my presumption that the dog was aware of certain of the circumstances that preceded it, and with other things I know about the situation. I want, in short, to provide an explanation that makes the dog's barking there now more or less reasonable in the light of the fact that it has just been chasing (what I know to be) a squirrel, that the dog saw the squirrel run up the tree at the base of which it is barking now, and that (as I have seen, but I think the dog has not), the squirrel is now in another tree. There are probably a lot of belief attributions that would fill the bill quite nicely. And I would probably be willing to agree that all of them adequately characterize, more or less, what the dog believes, even though the sentences in question differ in meaning from one another. I am also prepared to admit that other explanations of the action will also be justified by the available data. But I don't think any of this robs attributing beliefs to infrahumans and infants of its point. Our explanations of the actions of adults, as well as of infants and infrahumans, are not 'covering law' explanations. They have a lot of built-in slack. But we are also capable of recognizing when a proffered explanation is in the running or not: namely, we are capable of recognizing when an explanation, and with it the attributed belief, renders the behaviour reasonable in the light of those of the surrounding circumstances of which we are aware.

Conclusion

I have argued that the truth of our common-sense beliefs to the effect that people act as they do because of what they believe and want, and that we inhabit a world of objects, situations, and events whose existence and features are independent of our perception of them and thought about them, is the best explanation of the differential performance of 3-year-olds and adults in experimental conditions and also in natural settings. Adults typically succeed in the actions they perform based on these beliefs. Younger children typically do not succeed in these same situations. The truth of the beliefs thus seems a well-grounded hypothesis to explain the difference in the behaviour of the two populations.

Of course, my argument will not convince the died-in-the-wool philosophical sceptic, who will point out that other hypotheses are available which are consistent with the available data. For instance, there is the hypothesis that we might be brains in a vat of nutrients, our afferent and efferent nerve endings stimulated by the high-tech descendant of Descartes's evil genius, so that it seems as though we perform certain actions which are successful, and so that it seems as though we observe young children failing to accomplish their goals in similar circumstances. We do not have Cartesian certainty that this hypothesis is not true, if it is a coherently intelligible hypothesis.[3] Also available, perhaps, are Berkeleyan subjective idealism, the various versions of phenomenalism, Lockean representational realism, and other views which have been claimed to be consistent with all the empirical data. Unlike Moore, who thought these were simply rival analyses of those common-sense propositions he called judgements of perception, and are not incompatible with common sense, I have argued that they are far from what we commonly believe about the world we perceive.

If mere consistency with the data is all that is needed intellectually to motivate scepticism with regard to our common-sense view, then scepticism is available as an intellectual exercise or parlour game. But scepticism was a serious challenge when it seemed to follow inevitably from a model of the mind that was thought to be indubitable: namely, the conviction that we are immediately cognizant only of our own thoughts (ideas, sense-data). In Chapters 6 and 7, through an examination of the arguments of Reid and Moore, we saw that this model of the mind is not the only model available. Its alleged indubitability in fact is an artefact of the conviction that the phenomenology of consciousness is a sure guide to the ontology of the mind, the conviction that what is phenomenologically obvious is true. If this model of the mind is abandoned in favour of a somewhat different representational model which does not reify representations, common-sense realism is no longer stigmatized as the view that leads inevitably to sceptical consequences.

Now since common-sense realism does express what we believe, and is in particular implicated in the beliefs that are involved in the actions in which we are successful in achieving our action goals, and these beliefs are absent in the unsuccessful actions of young children in the same or similar circumstances, it seems to be the most natural, the simplest, explanation of our success. Surely no one can be thought naïve or insufficiently critical for believing it. It is no less sophisticated than its rivals, which were in any case invented and developed in detail to give alternative explanations of what was, erroneously, thought to be a hopeless doctrine.

The truth of common-sense realism, then, cannot be *demonstrated*; but I hope that I have shown that it is a plausible and workable theorette which explains why we get along in the world as well as we do, and why infants and young children, fortunately only temporarily, do not.

Notes

1 What is common sense?

1. For variety, I will sometimes refer to epistemic states simply as *beliefs*, and to desiderative states simply as *desires* or *wants*.
2. References to Aristotle are to Book, Section, and numbered Sentence of *The Nicomachean Ethics*. Quotations are from the translation of H. Rackham (Cambridge, MA: Harvard University Press, 1962).
3. This is basically the view defended by Donald Davidson (1975, 1982). I shall take up this criticism in Chapter 8.
4. Berkeley's view will be outlined in more detail in Chapter 5.
5. See Chisholm (1948) and Berlin (1950) for arguments to this effect.
6. The argument of this paragraph owes much to my reading of S. A. Grave (1960), who distinguishes between the empirical content and the metaphysical content of common-sense propositions, and argues that some philosophers think they are capturing what these propositions really mean when they offer an account which captures, at best, the empirical content. 'Why do most men resist the analyses of common sense beliefs put forward by phenomenalists or positivists? ... When told, "This is the sort of thing you really mean", why do they not say "Yes, that is the sort of thing I really mean"? They have it patiently explained to them, for example, that the philosopher is not telling them that there are no tables; that on the contrary, he is telling them what tables are. They are unimpressed. They do not think that "There are tables, and they are clusters of sensations" is any better than "There are no tables, only clusters of sensations." The phenomenalistic analyses are rejected by most men as soon as they are proposed and understood, and if suspected of being phenomenalistic, before they are understood.' From S. A. Grave (1960: 108). Berlin (1950) also argues in a similar vein.
7. Though it is not, of course, a truth condition of the sentence thereby asserted: it's the act of asserting that presupposes the belief for its intelligibility. This account of 'Moore's paradox' was first advanced in Forguson (1969). Moore's own discussion appears in Moore (1912).
8. This claim would be disputed by those, particularly anthropologists who have studied exotic cultures, who think that the linguistic and social differences between cultures are in some cases so extreme as to amount to 'incommensurable conceptual frameworks'. But my

imputation of a universal underlying common-sense view focuses on very mundane features of everyday individual and social existence that, I think, are unaffected by extremely wide variations in linguistic structure and social organization. In this I agree with Donald Davidson's (1974) argument that our ability to interpret the speech of others as the meaningful utterances of rational creatures, rather than mere noises made by brutes, presupposes that we share with them a vast underlying framework of shared beliefs about the world. It is only against the background of shared beliefs, he argues, that differences and disagreements will be discoverable. I explore some aspects of Davidson's theory of 'radical interpretation' in Chapter 8.

9. I have inserted the parenthetical 'roughly' in both cases to acknowledge that the agent might want something more than x, even though she wants x; that the agent might think that some action A might be even more effective in bringing it about that x obtain; and hosts of other qualifications which would be needed for technical nicety.

10. This point, as well as the one discussed in the previous paragraph, was suggested to me by Ausonio Marras in his comments, at the 1987 Canadian Philosophical Association, on an earlier version of Forguson and Gopnik (1988), which I presented at that conference.

11. The foregoing section owes a great deal to David Lewis (1972), and to Henry Wellman (1988). Wellman, also influenced by Lewis, identifies the holistic connections among theoretical terms in explanatory theories, and identifies common-sense psychology as embodying a theory-like structure featuring ontological distinctions in terms of which coherent explanations of behaviour are provided.

2 Common sense and metarepresentation

1. Remember, to represent something as a feature of the world does not imply that there really is any such feature of the world 'outside' one's current representation.

2. The controversy over the ontological status of sensory representations has died down almost completely since the debate following the publication of J. L. Austin's *Sense and Sensibilia* (1962), and the celebrated attack mounted in that book against the existence of sense-data. Critics and defenders of sense-data had their say in the journals for a few years. Since then, relatively little has been said on the topic, as the centre of the debate shifted to the philosophy of mind. I joined Austin's side in the sense-data bashing in Forguson (1969a).

3. For surveys of the fairly recent (and burgeoning) literature on the subject of beliefs and other non-sensory representations, see Fodor (1985) and Bogdan (1986). Baker (1987) has recently mounted a sustained defence of the realist position. Prominent among the eliminativists are P. M. Churchland (1979, 1981, 1984) and P. S. Churchland (1986). Instrumentalist views have been advanced by Davidson (1980) and Dennett (1978, 1987).

178

4. But if there really are no mental representations, then there really are no beliefs. But if there really are no beliefs, then, as Baker (1987) points out, this is going to have pretty disturbing consequences in semantics. For if there are no beliefs, then what are we to make of the English sentence 'There are no beliefs'? It might also be pointed out that truth is not merely a property of sentences, it is a relation among sentences, people, and times. 'There are no beliefs' is true if and only if, as uttered by S at t, there are no beliefs. But a noise (or inscription) is a token of a sentence type only if it is uttered as conforming to the rules of some language L. For S to utter a token of 'There are no beliefs' as conforming to L, presumably he must believe that 'There are no beliefs' conforms to L, or will be interpreted as conforming to L by others. And to interpret 'There are no beliefs' as being a token of the English language sentence-type 'There are no beliefs', is presumably to come to believe that it does. But if there are no beliefs, how can any of this be?

5. We don't, however, very often use *canonical* mental-representation attribution sentences to do so. Usually our attribution of mental representations to others is done via the utterance of sentences which, though not canonical, are synonymous with some canonical mental-representation attribution sentence.

6. My use of the expression 'mental representation' has many similarities with Descartes's technical term 'thought' (Fr. *pensée*; L. *cogitatione*), as he explains its use in *Meditations* III. Though he makes it clear that he is attempting to describe the results of a phenomenological (or introspective) survey of the contents of his mind, the logical features of thoughts parallel quite closely my characterization of mental representations. Thoughts, he tells us, are made up of a mental *act* (e.g. affirming, denying, perceiving [in the narrow sense of sensing, or seemingly perceiving], wanting, etc.), the object of which is an *idea*. I discuss this further in Chapter 5.

7. For a probing examination of some of these difficulties, see Donald Davidson (1975, 1982). See also Norman Malcolm (1973), and two books by Jonathan Bennett (1964, 1976). I shall return to this issue in Chapter 8.

4 The origins of common sense: the representational model of the mind

1. Note that 'concrete' and 'abstract' do no work in Leslie's account: in fact, a mentally represented unicorn, or a mentally represented banana-as-telephone, are as concrete, or at least as particular, as any material entity. The difference between material and immaterial things is not one of concrete vs. abstract, but simply of material vs. not material.

2. They do not, of course, recognize them as mental representations in the sense that they would make use of, or even understand, the technical vocabulary of mental representation. I mean only that they recognize themselves and others as being in states which are satisfied

if and only if the world is, or were to be, a certain way. They attribute to themselves and to others what we, but not they, call mental representations, in that they attribute false beliefs, recognize that things look differently to others than to themselves, etc.

5 Representation and scepticism

1. References to Descartes's *Discourse on Method* are to the numbered Parts. References to the *Meditations* are to the numbered Meditations. References to the *Principles of Philosophy* are to the numbered Parts and Principles. All quotations are from *The Philosophical Works of Descartes*, translated by E. S. Haldane and G. R. T. Ross, 2 volumes (Cambridge, UK: Cambridge University Press, 1969).
2. All references to Locke's *Essay Concerning Human Understanding* are to Book, Chapter, and Section in the edition of A. C. Fraser (Oxford: Oxford University Press, 1894).
3. References to Berkeley's *A Treatise Concerning the Principles of Human Knowledge* are to the numbered paragraphs. The quotations are from the edition of C. Turbayne (New York: Bobbs-Merrill, 1957).
4. All references to Hume's *Treatise of Human Nature* are to Book, Chapter, and Section in the standard edition of L. A. Selby-Bigge (Oxford: Oxford University Press, 1951).

6 Thomas Reid's defence of common sense

1. References are to Chapter and Section numbers in *An Inquiry into the Human Mind on the Principles of Common Sense*, and to Essay, Chapter, and Section numbers in *Essays on the Intellectual Powers of Man*. All quotations are from *The Works of Thomas Reid*, edited by Sir William Hamilton, sixth edition, 1863.
2. Actually, Locke wavered between a basically rationalist account of perceptual knowledge, in which the existence and characteristics of external things is inferred from our ideas, and a causal account of the process of perception, according to which objects in the world cause modifications in our minds (the ideas) by means of which we perceive the objects directly. The former account he inherited from Descartes; in the latter he was influenced by the physics and physiology of his day. But his insistence on the Cartesian model effectively prevented him from developing the causal account in a way which could be integrated with his epistemology.
3. This is not to say that we are totally bereft of a common-sense understanding of the causal conditions of perception. As we saw in Chapter 3, even very young children have a pretty fair idea of the conditions that have to obtain for someone to visually perceive something.

7 G. E. Moore: direct realism and common sense

1. This paper was originally published in 1925. It was reprinted in G. E. Moore, *Philosophical Papers* (London: Macmillan, 1959). References in parentheses are to page numbers in *Philosophical Papers*
2. This paper was originally published in 1918. It was reprinted in G. E. Moore, *Philosophical Studies* (London: Routledge & Kegan Paul, 1922). References in parentheses are to the page numbers in *Philosophical Studies*.
3. A similar argument was used by Moore in a series of lectures he gave in 1910–11, but not published until more than forty years later. See Chapter 6 of Moore's *Some Main Problems of Philosophy* (London: Allen & Unwin, 1953).

8 A defence of common sense

1. This has been effectively pointed out by, among others, Dennett (1978) and Davidson (1980).
2. Davidson (1977) has argued similarly in defence of a theory of radical interpretation based on a Tarski-style theory of truth as an empirically adequate explanation of linguistic behaviour.
3. Putnam (1981) has argued it is not intelligible.

Bibliography

Aksu-Koc, A. A. and Slobin, D. I. (1986) 'The Acquisition of Turkish' in
D. I. Slobin (ed.) *The Cross-Linguistic Study of Language
Acquisition*, Hillsdale, NJ: Lawrence Erlbaum & Associates.

Aristotle (1962) *Nicomachean Ethics*, translated by H. Rackham,
Cambridge, MA: Harvard University Press.

Astington, J. W. (in press) 'Intention in the Child's Theory of Mind' in C.
Moore and D. Frye (eds.) *Children's Theories of Mind*, Hillsdale, NJ:
Lawrence Erlbaum & Associates.

Astington, J. W., Harris, P. L., and Olson, D. R. (eds.) (1988)
Developing Theories of Mind, Cambridge, UK: Cambridge University
Press.

Astington, J. W. and Gopnik, A. (1988) 'Knowing You've Changed
Your Mind: Children's Understanding of Representational Change' in
J. W. Astington, P. Harris, and D. Olson (eds.) *Developing Theories
of Mind*, Cambridge, UK: Cambridge University Press.

Austin, J. L. (1962) *Sense and Sensibilia*, reconstructed from the
manuscript notes and edited by G. J. Warnock, Oxford: Oxford
University Press.

Ayer, A. J. (1940) *The Foundations of Empirical Knowledge*, London:
Macmillan.

Baker, J. R. (1987) *Saving Belief: A Critique of Physicalism*, Princeton,
NJ: Princeton University Press.

Bates, E., Camaioni, L., and Volterra, V. (1975) 'The Acquisition of
Performatives Prior to Speech', *Merrill-Palmer Quarterly* 21: 205–26.

Beal, C. R. and Flavell, J. H. (1984) 'Development of the Ability to
Distinguish Communicative Intention and Literal Message Meaning',
Child Development 55: 920–8.

Bennett, J. (1964) *Rationality*, London: Routledge and Kegan Paul.

Bennett, J. (1976) *Linguistic Behaviour*, Cambridge, UK: Cambridge
University Press.

Berkeley, G. (1957) *A Treatise Concerning the Principles of Human
Knowledge*, edited by C. Turbayne, New York: Bobbs-Merrill. First
published in 1710.

Berlin, I. (1950) 'Empirical Propositions and Hypothetical Statements',
Mind 59: 289–312.

Bloom, L., Lightbown, P., and Hood, L. (1975) 'Structure and Variation in Child Language', *Monographs of the Society for Research on Child Development* 40.

Bogdan, R. J. (1986) *Belief: Form, Content and Function*, Oxford: Clarendon Press.

Bowerman, M. (1976) 'Semantic Factors in the Acquisition of Rules for Word Use and Sentence Construction' in D. M. Moorhead and A. E. Moorhead (eds.) *Normal and Deficient Child Language* Baltimore: University Park Press.

Braine, M. D. S. and Shanks, B. L. (1965) 'The Development of Conservation of Size', *Journal of Verbal Learning and Verbal Behavior* 4: 227–42.

Bretherton, I., McNew, S., and Beeghly-Smith, M. (1981) 'Early Person Knowledge as Expressed in Gestural and Verbal Communication: When Do Infants Acquire a "Theory of Mind"?' in M. E. Lamb and L. R. Sherod (eds.) *Infant Social Cognition*, Hillsdale, NJ: Lawrence Erlbaum & Associates.

Bretherton, I. and Beeghly, M. (1982) 'Talking about Internal States: the Acquisition of an Explicit Theory of Mind', *Developmental Psychology* 18: 906–21.

Broad, C. D. (1923) *Scientific Thought*, New York: Harcourt Brace.

Brown, R. (1973) *A First Language: The Early Stages*, Cambridge, MA: Harvard University Press.

Bruner, J. S. (1975) 'The Ontogenesis of Speech Acts', *Journal of Child Language* 2: –19.

Chandler, M. (1988) 'Doubt and Developong Theories of Mind' in J. W. Astington, P. L. Harris, and D. R. Olson (eds.) *Developing Theories of Mind*, Cambridge, UK: Cambridge University Press.

Chandler, M. and Helm, D. (1984) 'Developmental Changes in the Contributions of Shared Experience to Social Role-Taking Competence', *International Journal of Behavioural Development* 7: 145–56.

Chisholm, R. (1948) 'The Problem of Empiricism', *Journal of Philosophy* 45: 512–17.

Chisholm, R. (1957) *Perceiving: A Philosophical Study*, Ithaca, NY: Cornell University Press.

Chomsky, N. (1980) *Rules and Representations*, New York: Columbia University Press.

Churchland, P. M. (1979) *Scientific Realism and the Plasticity of Mind*, Cambridge, UK: Cambridge University Press.

Churchland, P. M. (1981) 'Eliminative Materialism and the Propositional Attitudes', *Journal of Philosophy* 78: 67–90.

Churchland, P. M. (1984) *Matter and Consciousness: A Contemporary Introduction to the Philosophy of Mind*, Cambridge, MA: MIT Press.

Churchland, P. S. (1986) *Neurophilosophy: Toward a Unified Theory of Mind/Brain*, Cambridge, MA: MIT Press.

Clinchy, B. and Mansfield, A. (1985) *Justifications Offered by Children to Support Positions on Issues of 'Fact' and 'Opinion'*, paper presented at the fifty-sixth annual meeting of the Eastern Psychological Association, Boston.

Davidson, D. (1974) 'On the Very Idea of a Conceptual Scheme', *Proceedings and Addresses of the American Philosophical Association* 47: 5–20, reprinted in Davidson (1984).

Davidson, D. (1975) 'Thought and Talk' in S. Guttenplan (ed.) *Mind and Language*, Oxford: Oxford University Press, reprinted in Davidson, (1984).

Davidson, D. (1977) 'Reality Without Reference', reprinted in Davidson (1984).

Davidson, D. (1980) *Essays on Action and Events*, Oxford: Clarendon Press.

Davidson, D. (1982) 'Rational Animals', *Dialectica*, 36: 318–27.

Davidson, D. (1984a) *Inquiries into Truth and Interpretation*, Oxford: Clarendon Press.

Davidson, D. (1984b) 'A Coherence Theory of Truth and Knowledge' in E. LePore (ed.) *Truth and Interpretation*, St. Paul, Minn.: University of Minnesota Press.

DeLoache, J. S. (1987) 'The Development of Representation in Young Children' in H. W. Reese (ed.) *Advances in Child Development and Behavior*, NY: Academic Press.

Dennett, D. C. (1978) *Brainstorms: Philosophical Essays on Mind and Psychology*, Montgomery, VT: Bradford Books.

Dennett, D. C. (1987) *The Intentional Stance*, Cambridge, MA: MIT Press.

Descartes, R. (1969) *The Philosophical Works of Descartes*, translated by E. S. Haldane and G. R. T. Ross, 2 volumes, Cambridge, UK: Cambridge University Press.

DeSousa, R. (1971) 'How to Give a Piece of Your Mind: or, the Logic of Belief and Assent', *Review of Metaphysics* 25: 52–79.

DeVries, R. (1970) 'The Development of Role-Taking as Reflected by the Behavior of Bright, Average, and Retarded Children in a Social Guessing Game', *Child Development* 41: 759–70.

DiSessa, A. (1985) 'Learning about Knowing', *New Directions for Child Development* 28: 97–124.

Dunn, J., Bretherton, I., and Munn, P. (1987) 'Conversations about Feeling States Between Mothers and Their Young Children', *Developmental Psychology* 23: 132–9.

Enright, R. and Lapsley, D. (1980) 'Social Role-Taking: a Review of the Construct, Measures, and Measurement Properties', *Review of Educational Research* 50: 647–74.

Enright, R., Lapsley, D., Franklin, C., and Steuck, K. (1984) 'Longitudinal and Cross-Cultural Validation of the Belief-Discrepancy Reasoning Construct', *Developmental Psychology* 20: 143–9.

Flavell, J. H. (1978) 'The Development of Knowledge about Visual Perception' in C. B. Keasy (ed.) *Nebraska Symposium on Motivation* (vol. 25, pp. 43–76), Lincoln: University of Nebraska Press.

Flavell, J. H. (1986) 'The Development of Children's Knowledge about the Appearance–Reality Distinction', *American Psychologist* 41: 418–25.

Flavell, J. H. (1988) 'The Development of Children's Knowledge about the Mind: from Cognitive Connections to Mental Representations' in J. W. Astington, P. L. Harris, and D. R. Olson (eds.) *Developing Theories of Mind*, Cambridge, UK: Cambridge University Press.

Flavell, J. H., Everett, B. A., Croft, K., and Flavell, E. R. (1981) 'Young Children's Knowledge about Visual Perception: Further Evidence for the Level 1–Level 2 Distinction', *Developmental Psychology* 17: 99–103.

Flavell, J. H., Flavell, E. R., Green, F. L., and Wilcox, S. A. (1980) 'Young Children's Knowledge about Visual Perception: Effect of Observer's Distance from Target on Perceptual Clarity of Target', *Developmental Psychology* 16: 10–12.

Flavell, J. H., Green, F. L., and Flavell, E. R. (1986) 'Development of Knowledge about the Appearance–Reality Distinction', *Monographs of the Society for Research in Child Development*, Serial No. 212,51 (1).

Flavell, J. H., Green, F. L., and Flavell, E. R. (unpublished manuscript) 'The Development of Children's Knowledge about the Mind: a Test of the Connections–Representations Theory'.

Flavell, J. H., Zhang, X.-D., Zhou, H., Qi, S., and Dong, Q. (1983) 'A Comparison Between the Development of the Appearance–Reality Distinction in The People's Republic of China and the United States', *Cognitive Psychology* 15: 459–66.

Fodor, J. R. (1975) *The Language of Thought*, Hassocks, UK: Harvester Press.

Fodor, J. R. (1985) 'Fodor's Guide to Mental Representations: an Intelligent Auntie's Vade Mecum', *Mind* 94: 76–100.

Fodor, J. R. (1987) *Psychosemantics*, Cambridge, MA: MIT Press.

Forguson, L. W. (1969a) 'Has Ayer Refuted the Sense-Datum Theory?' in K. T. Fann (ed.) *Symposium on J. L. Austin*, London: Routledge and Kegan Paul.

Forguson, L. W. (1969b) 'On "It's Raining But I Don't Believe It" ', *Theoria* 7: 89–101.

Forguson, L. W. (1987) 'Common Sense and Perception in the Philosophy of G. E. Moore', in F. van Holtoon and D. Olson (eds.) *Common Sense: The Foundations for Social Science*, New York: University Press of America.

Forguson, L. W. and Gopnik, A. (1988) 'The Ontogeny of Common Sense' in J. W. Astington, P. L. Harris, and D. R. Olson (eds.) *Developing Theories of Mind*, Cambridge, UK: Cambridge University Press.

Gardner, D., Harris, P. L., Ohmoto, M., and Hamazaki, T. (in press) 'Understanding of the Distinction Between Real and Apparent Emotion by Japanese Children', *International Journal of Behavioral Development*.

Golinkoff, R. M. and Harding, C. G. (1980) *Infant's Expectations of the Movement Potential of Inanimate Objects*, paper presented at the International Conference on Infant Studies, New Haven, CT.

Goodman, N. (1968) *Languages of Art*, New York: Bobbs-Merrill.

Bibliography

Gopnik, A. (1982) 'Words and Plans: Early Language and the Development of Intelligent Action', *Journal of Child Language* 9: 303–18.

Gopnik, A. (1984a) 'Conceptual and Semantic Change in Scientists and Children: Why There are No Semantic Universals', *Linguistics* 20: 163–79.

Gopnik, A. (1984b) 'The Acquisition of *Gone* and the Development of the Object Concept', *Journal of Child Language* 11: 273–92.

Gopnik, A. and Astington, J. W. (1988) 'Children's Understanding of Representational Change and its Relation to the Understanding of False Belief and the Appearance–Reality Distinction', *Child Development* 59: 26–37.

Gopnik, A. and Graf, P. (1988)' Knowing How You Know: Children's Understanding of the Sources of their Beliefs', *Child Development* 59: 1366–7.

Gopnik, A. and Meltzoff, A. N. (1984) 'Semantic and Cognitive Development in 15- to 21-Month-Old Children', *Journal of Child Language* 11: 495–513.

Gopnik, A. and Meltzoff, A. N. (1985a) 'From People, to Plans, to Objects: Changes in the Meaning of Early Words and their Relation to Cognitive Development', *Journal of Pragmatics* 9: 495–512.

Gopnik, A. and Meltzoff, A. N. (1985b) 'Language, Thought, and their Interaction During the First Two Years of Childhood: the Cognitive-Developmental Hypothesis' in S. A. Kuczaj II and M. D. Barrett (eds.) *The Development of Word Meaning*, New York: Springer Verlag.

Gopnik, A. and Meltzoff, A. N. (1985c) 'Words, Plans, Things, and Locations: Interactions Between Semantic and Cognitive Development in the One-Word Stage' in S. A. Kuczaj II and M. D. Barrett (eds.) *The Development of Word Meaning*, New York: Springer Verlag.

Gopnik, A. and Meltzoff, A. N. (1986) 'Relationships Between Semantic and Cognitive Development in the One-Word Stage: the Specificity Hypothesis', *Child Development* 57: 1040–53.

Gopnik, A. and Meltzoff, A. N. (1987) 'Language and Thought in the Young Child: Early Semantic Developments and their Relationship to Object Permanence, Means–Ends Understanding, and Categorization', in K. Nelson and A. van Kleeck (eds.) *Children's Language* vol. 6, Hillsdale, NJ: Lawrence Erlbaum & Associates.

Gratch, G. (1964) 'Response Alternation in Children: a Developmental Study of Orientations to Uncertainty', *Vita Humana* 7: 49–60.

Grave, S. A. (1960) *The Scottish Philosophy of Common Sense*, Oxford: Clarendon Press.

Harris, P. L., Donnelly, K., Guz, G. R., and Pitt-Watson, R. (1986) 'Children's Understanding of the Distinction Between Real and Apparent Emotion', *Child Development* 57: 895–909.

Harris, P. L., Gardner, D., and Gross, D. (1987) *Children's Understanding of Real and Apparent Emotion*, paper presented at the Society for Research in Child Development, Baltimore, MD.

Harris, P. L. and Gross, D. (1988) 'Children's Understanding of Real and Apparent Emotion' in J. W. Astington, P. L. Harris, and D. Olson (eds.) *Developing Theories of Mind*, New York: Cambridge University Press.

Hogrefe, G. -J., Wimmer, H., and Perner, J. (1986) 'Ignorance Versus False Belief: a Developmental Lag in Attribution of Epistemic States', *Child Development* 57: 567–82.

Hood, L. and Bloom, L. (1979) 'What, When, and How About Why: a Longitudinal Study of Early Expression of Causality', *Monograph of the Society for Research in Child Development*, serial No. 181.

Hume, D. (1951) *A Treatise of Human Nature*, edited by L. A. Selby-Bigge, Oxford: Oxford University Press. Originally published in three volumes, 1738–40.

Johnson, C. N. (1982) 'Acquisition of Mental Verbs and the Concept of Mind' in S. A. Kuczaj II (ed.) *Language Development: Syntax and Semantics*, Hillside, NJ: Lawrence Erlbaum & Associates.

Johnson, C. N. and Wellman, H. M. (1982) 'Children's Developing Conceptions of the Mind and Brain', *Child Development* 53: 222–34.

Kripke, S. (1972) *Naming and Necessity*, Cambridge, MA: Harvard University Press.

Kuhn, D., Pennington, N., and Leadbeater, B. (1983) 'Adult Thinking in Developmental Perspective' in P. Baltes and O. Brim Jr. (eds.) *Life-span Development and Behavior*, New York: Academic Press.

La Frenière, P. J. (1988) 'The Ontogeny of Tactical Deception in Humans' in R. W. Byrne and A. Whiten (eds.) *Machiavellian Intelligence: Social Expertise and the Evolution of Intellect: in Monkeys, Apes and Humans*, Oxford: Clarendon Press, 238–52.

Leekam, S. R. and Perner, J. (1987: unpublished manuscript) 'Belief and Disbelief: Young Children's Conception of the Mind as an Active Processor of Information'.

Lempers, J. D., Flavell, E. R., and Flavell, J. H. (1977) 'The Development in Very Young Children of Tacit Knowledge Concerning Visual Perception', *Genetic Psychology Monographs* 95: 3–53.

Leslie, A. M. (1987) 'Pretence and Representation: the Origins of "Theory of Mind" ', *Psychological Review* 94: 412–26.

Leslie, A. M. (1988) 'Some Implications of Pretense for Mechanisms Underlying the Child's Theory of Mind' in J. W. Astington, P. L. Harris, and D. R. Olson (eds.) *Developing Theories of Mind*, Cambridge, UK: Cambridge University Press.

Lewis, C. I. (1947) *An Analysis of Knowledge and Valuation*, La Salle, Illinois: Open Court.

Lewis, D. (1972) 'Psychophysical and Theoretical Identifications', *Australasian Journal of Philosophy* 50: 249–58.

Locke, J. (1894) *Essay Concerning Human Understanding*, edited by A. C. Fraser, 2 volumes, Oxford: Oxford University Press. Originally published in 1689.

Malcolm, N. (1973) 'Thoughtless Brutes', *Proceedings and Addresses of the American Philosophical Association* 46:5–20.

187

Maratsos, M. P. (1973) 'Nonegocentric Communication Abilities in Preschool Children', *Child Development* 44: 697–700.

Marvin, R. S., Greenberg, M. T., and Mossler, D. G. (1976) 'The Early Development of Conceptual Perspective-Taking: Distinguishing Among Multiple Perspectives', *Child Development* 45: 511–14.

Masangkay, Z. S., McCluskey, K. A., McIntyre, C. W., Sims-Knight, J., Vaughn, B. E., and Flavell, J. H. (1974) 'The Early Development of Inferences About the Visual Percepts of Others', *Child Development* 45: 357–66.

Mill, J. S. (1872) *An Examination of Sir William Hamilton's Philosophy*, fourth edition, London: Longmans, Green, Reader & Dyer.

Moore, G. E. (1912) *Ethics*, London: Williams and Norgate.

Moore, G. E. (1922a) 'The Refutation of Idealism' in G. E. Moore, *Philosophical Studies*, London: Routledge and Kegan Paul. Paper originally published in 1903.

Moore, G. E. (1922b) 'Some Judgments of Perception' in G. E. Moore, *Philosophical Studies*, London: Routledge and Kegan Paul. Paper originally published in 1918.

Moore, G. E. (1953) *Some Main Problems of Philosophy*, London: Allen & Unwin.

Moore, G. E. (1959) 'A Defence of Common Sense' in G. E. Moore, *Philosophical Papers*, London: Allen & Unwin. Paper originally published in 1925.

Mossler, D. G., Marvin, R. S., and Greenberg, M. T. (1976) 'Conceptual Perspective-Taking in 2- to 6-Year Old Children', *Developmental Psychology* 12: 85–6.

Olson, D. R. (1977) 'From Utterance to Text: the Bias of Language in Speech and Writing', *Harvard Educational Review* 47: 257–81.

Olson, D. R. (unpublished manuscript) 'Representation and Misrepresentation: on the Beginnings of Symbolization in Young Children'.

Olson, D. R. and Astington, J. W. (1987) 'Seeing and Knowing: on the Ascription of Mental States to Young Children', *Canadian Journal of Psychology* 41: 399–411.

Olson, D. R. and Hildyard, A. (1983) 'Literacy and the Comprehension and Expression of Literal Meaning', in F. Coulmas and K. Ehlich (eds.) *Writing in Focus,* New York: Mouton.

Perner, J. (1988a) 'Developing Semantics for Theories of Mind: from Propositional attitudes to Mental Representations' in J. W. Astington. P. L. Harris, and D. R. Olson (eds.) *Developing Theories of Mind,* Cambridge, UK: Cambridge University Press.

Perner, J. (1988b) 'Higher-Order Beliefs and Intentions in Children's Understanding of Social Interaction' in J. W. Astington, P. L. Harris, and D. R. Olson (eds.) *Developing Theories of Mind*, Cambridge, UK: Cambridge University Press.

Perner, J., Leekam, S., and Wimmer, H. (1987) 'Three-Year-Olds' Difficulty With False Belief: the Case for a Conceptual Deficit', *British Journal of Developmental Psychology* 5: 125–37.

Piaget, J. (1951) *Play, Dreams and Imitation in Childhood,* New York: Norton.

Pillow, B. H. and Flavell, J. H. (1986) 'Young Children's Knowledge About Visual Perception: Projective Size and Shape', *Child Development* 57: 125–35.

Poulin-Dubois, D. and Shultz, T. R. (1988) 'The Development of the Understanding of Human Behavior: from Agency to Intentionality' in J. W. Astington, P. L. Harris, and D. R. Olson (eds.) *Developing Theories of Mind*, Cambridge, UK: Cambridge University Press.

Price, H. H. (1940) *Hume's Theory of the External World*, Oxford: Oxford University Press.

Putnam, H. (1981) *Reason, Truth and History*, Cambridge, UK: Cambridge University Press.

Reid, T. (1863) *The Works of Thomas Reid*, ed. Sir William Hamilton, 6th edition, Edinburgh: Maclachlan and Stewart; London: Longman, Roberts, & Green.

Robinson, E. J. and Robinson, W. P. (1982) 'Knowing When You Don't Know Enough: Children's Judgments About Ambiguous Information', *Cognition* 12: 267–80.

Russell, B. (1917) *Mysticism and Logic*, London: Allen and Unwin.

Russell, J. (1988) 'Making Judgments About Thoughts and Things' in J. W. Astington, P. L. Harris, and D. R. Olson (eds.) *Developing Theories of Mind*, Cambridge, UK: Cambridge University Press.

Scaife, M. and Bruner, J. S. (1975) 'The Capacity for Joint Visual Attention in the Infant', *Nature* 253: 265–6.

Searle, J. (1983) *Intentionality: an Essay in the Philosophy of Mind*, Cambridge, UK: Cambridge University Press.

Shatz, M., Wellman, H. M., and Silber, S. (1983) 'The Acquisition of Mental Verbs: a Systematic Investigation of the First Reference to Mental State', *Cognition* 14: 301–21.

Shultz, T. R. (1980) 'Development of the Concept of Intention' in W. A. Collins (ed.) *The Minnesota Symposium on Child Psychology* vol. 13. Hillsdale, NJ : Lawrence Erlbaum & Associates.

Shultz, T. R. (1988) 'Assessing Intention: a Computational Model' in J. W. Astington, P. L. Harris, and D. R. Olson (eds.) *Developing Theories of Mind*, Cambridge, UK: Cambridge University Press.

Shultz, T. R. and Cloghesy, K. (1981) 'Development of Recursive Awareness of Intention', *Developmental Psychology* 17: 465–71.

Shultz, T. R. and Wells, D. (1985) 'Judging the Intentionality of Action-Outcomes', *Developmental Psychology* 21: 83–9.

Slobin, D. I. (1970) 'Universals of Grammatical Development in Children' in G. B. Flores d'Arcais and W. J. M. Levelt (eds.) *Advances in Psycholinguistics*, New York: Elsevier.

Smith, M. C. (1978) 'Cognizing the Behavior Stream: the Recognition of Intentional Action', *Child Development* 49: 736–43.

Sodian, B. (1988) 'Children's Attribution of Knowledge to the Listener in a Referential Communication Task', *Child Development* 59: 378–85.

Stich, S. (1983) *Fron Folk Psychology to Cognitive Science: the Case against Belief*, Cambridge, MA: MIT Press, A Bradford Book.

Taylor, M. (1988) 'The Development of Children's Understanding of the Seeing–Knowing Distinction' in J. W. Astington, P. L. Harris and D. R. Olson (eds.) *Developing Theories of Mind,* Cambridge, UK: Cambridge University Press.

Trevarthen, C. (1980) 'The Foundations of Intersubjectivity: Development of Interpersonal and Cooperative Understanding in Infancy' in D. Olson (ed.) *The Social Foundations of Language and Thought: Essays in Honor of J. S. Bruner*, NY: Norton.

Trevarthen, C. and Hubley, P. (1979) 'Secondary Intersubjectivity: Confidence, Confiding, and Acts of Meaning in the First Year' in A. Lock (ed.) *Action, Gesture and Symbol*, NY: Academic Press.

Wellman, H. M. (1985) 'The Origins of Metacognition' in D. L. Forrest-Pressley, G. E. MacKinnon, and T. G. Waller (eds.) *Metacognition, Cognition and Human Performance*, NY: Academic Press.

Wellman, H. M. (1988) 'First Steps in the Child's Theorizing about the Mind' in J. W. Astington, P. L. Harris, and D. R. Olson (eds.) *Developing Theories of Mind*, Cambridge, UK: Cambridge University Press.

Wellman, H. M. and Bartsch, K. (in press) 'Young Children's Reasoning About Beliefs', *Cognition.*

Wellman, H. M. and Estes, D. (1986) 'Early Understanding of Mental Entities: a Re-examination of Childhood Realism', *Child Development* 57: 910–23.

Wells, D. and Shultz, T. R. (1980) 'Developmental Distinctions Between Behavior and Judgments in the Operation of the Discounting Principle', *Child Development* 51: 1307–10.

Wimmer, H. and Perner, J. (1983) 'Beliefs About Beliefs: Representation and Constraining Function of Wrong Beliefs in Young Children's Understanding of Deception', *Cognition* 13: 103–28.

Wimmer, H., Hogrefe, J., and Sodian, B. (1988) 'A Second Stage in Children's Conception of Mental Life: Understanding Sources of Information' in J. W. Astington, P. L. Harris, and D. R. Olson (eds.) *Developing Theories of Mind*, Cambridge, UK: Cambridge University Press.

Wolf, D., Rygh, J., and Altshuler, J. (1984) 'Agency and Experience: Actions and States in Play Narratives' in I. Bretherton (ed.) *Symbolic Play*, NY: Academic Press.

Yaniv, I. and Shatz, M. (1988) 'Children's Understanding of Perceptibility' in J. W. Astington, P. L. Harris, and D. R. Olson (eds.) *Developing Theories of Mind*, Cambridge, UK: Cambridge University Press.

Index